LOCOMOTION PAPERS

Th_
Vale of Glamorgan
Railway

by
Colin Chapman

THE OAKWOOD PRESS

British Library Cataloguing in Publication Data
A Record for this book is available from the British Library
ISBN 0 85361 523 3

Typeset by Oakwood Graphics.
Repro by Ford Graphics, Ringwood, Hants.
Printed by Pheon Press Ltd, Whitchurch, Bristol.

Class '37' Co-Co No. 37 895 hauls a diverted steel train round the curve to the west of Aberthaw in 1996.   *R.H. Marrows*

Title Page: A diverted express hauled by 'Castle' class 4-6-0 No. 7027 *Thornbury Castle* at Aberthaw in 1957. Aberthaw Power Station can be seen under construction at The Leys in the background.   *R.O. Tuck*

Published by
The Oakwood Press
P.O. Box 13, Usk, Mon., NP5 1YS.

Contents

	Introduction	5
Chapter One	Prelude	7
Chapter Two	Promotion	11
Chapter Three	Construction and Inspection	29
Chapter Four	Celebration and Despair	41
Chapter Five	Unfulfilled Ambitions	47
Chapter Six	Independent Days	55
Chapter Seven	Under the Great Western	69
Chapter Eight	The British Railways Era	81
Chapter Nine	Locomotive and Train Working	95
Chapter Ten	Along the Line	131
Chapter Eleven	Hope Springs Eternal	167
Appendix One	Principal Acts of Parliament	173
Appendix Two	Shipment coal handed to the Vale of Glamorgan Railway 1897-1914	174
Appendix Three	Loads of Engines between Barry and Coity Junction, 11th July, 1914	175
	Acknowledgements	176
	Sources and Bibliography	176

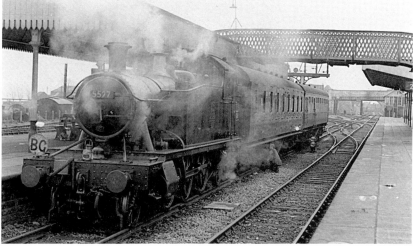

'55XX' 2-6-2T No. 5527 with the 2.08 pm (SO) auto-train to Bridgend, at Barry on 18th April, 1957. *S. Rickard Collection/Copyright B.J. Miller*

LLANTWIT MAJOR

W 1036

Author's Collection

The church of St Illtud and the old town of Llantwit Major viewed from the west.

Introduction

For most of the 19th century the Vale of Glamorgan remained untouched by the rapid and extensive development of the railway system which occurred elsewhere in South Wales. Indeed, it was not an obvious or an easy place in which to build railways. There was little, apart from its agricultural wealth and limestone resources, to attract the attention of railway companies or speculators, and there was never sufficient support available for the successful promotion of locally-based schemes. In addition, the terrain of much of the area was not particularly sympathetic to the activities of railway engineers. As a result, the 'Vale' remained something of a transport backwater, increasingly isolated and deprived of the actual and perceived benefits of connection to the growing railway network of South Wales. When railways eventually came to the Vale they were the product of outside forces and influences, with the needs of the local communities being very much a secondary consideration.

The term 'Vale' is clearly something of a misnomer, implying as it does a river valley between areas of higher ground. At the same time, definitions of its extent can vary, but the 'true' Vale is generally taken to be the rolling low plateau to the south of the central ridge, now occupied by the A48 road, between Cardiff and Bridgend. Although this includes the rural area to the east of Barry, the focus in this study will be on the country between Barry and Bridgend.

The geology of the Vale of Glamorgan has played a very important role in the development of its present character and appearance. For the most part it consists of alternate beds of lias limestone and thinner shale, with clay overlying this strata in river valleys. To the west, near St Bride's Major, this pattern is replaced by the more massive beds of older carboniferous limestone. The landscape tends to reflect this distinction, with the rolling plateau of the lias limestone country giving way to hillier ground in the west. The Vale is drained by two main river systems, the Thaw, which breaks through the central ridge at Llandough, about ½ mile south of Cowbridge, before flowing through a broad valley to the sea at Aberthaw, and the Ewenni and Alun, in the west.

The settlement pattern of the Vale of Glamorgan was characterised by an even spread of small villages and hamlets, with the small town (in the sense that it possessed a 'Town Hall', if not a charter) of Llantwit Major, midway between Barry and Bridgend, forming the largest centre of population. Llantwit Major, an anglicised form of the Welsh 'Llanilltud Fawr' - the great church of Illtud - was renowned as a centre of early Celtic Christianity, and was an attraction for earnest antiquary and casual tourist alike. Writing in March 1869, Thomas Jones, a resident of the town, noted that the average number of strangers occupying its lodgings during the previous bathing season had exceeded 400-500 persons per week. However, as a focus for trade and community life, Llantwit Major displayed a somewhat decayed rustic appearance and pace of life, and was always overshadowed by the neighbouring town of Cowbridge, about five miles to the north. Cowbridge was the dominant market and administrative centre not only for the central part of the Vale, but also for the large rural area to the north.

About four miles to the east of Llantwit Major was the small harbour of Aberthaw, at the mouth of the River Thaw. In pre-industrial days Aberthaw had been the most significant port in south Glamorgan, with important coastal and cross-channel links, but had quickly been eclipsed by the development of modern ports, such as Cardiff and Penarth from the middle of the 19th century. By the last quarter of the century it saw little traffic.

The historic core of Llantwit Major, looking towards the town square, *c.* 1910.

Author's Collection

Chapter One

Prelude

The combination of settlement pattern, limited traffic potential and topography found in the Vale of Glamorgan was not entirely conducive to railway promotion. Nevertheless, there had been some faint stirrings in the era of horse-drawn tramroads, which preceded the development of modern railways in South Wales. On 26th November, 1814 a meeting at the Wyndham Hotel, Bridgend, had approved of the suggestion that 'a tramroad from the hills north of Bridgend to Ewenny might be of great public utility'. Plans for this line were deposited for the 1815 Parliamentary Session, but the Bill was not proceeded with. Consideration was then given to an alternative proposal involving a route to the sea at the mouth of the River Ogmore, but this was formally abandoned on 16th April, 1816. An attempted revival of this scheme in 1818 also ended in failure, after which attention was redirected towards the harbour at Porthcawl. This led to the incorporation, in 1825, of the Duffryn Llynvi and Porth Cawl Railway (DL&PCR), and its opening, as a 4 ft 7 in. gauge 'edgeway', on 22nd June, 1828. In 1826 an abortive attempt was made to promote a tramroad from Trecastle Colliery, near Pontyclun, through Cowbridge to Aberthaw. One local scheme which did bear fruit was the Bridgend Railway, providing a link between the DL&PCR at Cefn Cribwr and Bridgend, which opened on 22nd October, 1830.

In addition, there was little hope of the development of through routes which might also have been of local benefit. The Roman road from Isca (Caerleon) to Moridunum (Carmarthen) had followed the central ridge, forming the northern limit to the Vale, passing through what later became Cowbridge. This route, with a number of diversions to avoid excessively steep gradients, formed the basis of the Cardiff-Swansea turnpike road created by Act of Parliament in 1764. The South Wales Railway (SWR), engineered by I.K. Brunel, and opened between Chepstow and Swansea on 18th June, 1850, avoided not only the 'true' Vale, but also most of the Border Vale to the north, by taking a broad arc as it followed the valleys of the Rivers Ely and Ewenni between Cardiff and Bridgend. Stations were provided at Llantrisant (known as 'Llantrissant' until about 1890, the town itself being about two miles to the north-east), Pencoed and Bridgend, but while these were well-placed for their immediate catchment areas, they served only a relatively small part of the rural hinterland to the south, with all three being about 10 miles from Llantwit Major.

The first railway to penetrate the rich agricultural district to the south of the SWR was the Cowbridge Railway (CR), incorporated by Act of 29th July, 1862. Opened to goods on 30th January, 1865, and to passengers on 18th September of that year, the CR was promoted by local interests, initially with support from the Taff Vale Railway (TVR), to connect the market town with the SWR at Llantrisant station, and, via the authorised Llantrissant and Taff Vale Junction Railway, to the heart of the TVR system at Pontypridd. It is clear that, from the outset, the Cowbridge promoters had ambitions to extend their railway down

7

the valley of the River Thaw to Aberthaw: writing in October 1862, Dr J.W. Nichol-Carne, a CR Director, stated, '. . . the promoters have every reason to believe that the railway will ultimately reach Aberthaw . . .'

By 1869 the inhabitants of Llantwit Major had become concerned that they were being left outside the growing railway system of South Wales. There was obvious scope for dissatisfaction with the existing transport facilities. At the time of the passing of the CR Act in 1862 a twice-weekly horse brake service linked Llantwit Major with Cardiff, via Cowbridge, taking four or five hours for the 18 mile journey. On 7th May, 1866, not long after the opening of the CR to passengers, David Wilde of Llantwit Major introduced a horse brake service, on Mondays and Wednesdays only, between his home town and Cowbridge station, in connection with the 7.45 am and 5.12 pm train departures and the 10.06 am and 8.34 pm arrivals. On Tuesdays, Thursdays and Fridays the conveyance was available for private hire, while on Saturdays it ran through to Cardiff, meeting the 8.34 pm arrival at Cowbridge station on its return. By 1871 this service, by then in the hands of one John Smith, was being worked on a daily basis, and was, with a variety of operators over the years, to become a long-standing feature of public transport in the Vale of Glamorgan.

Cowbridge also provided the natural focus for early ideas for a railway to connect Llantwit Major with the outside world. On 15th February, 1869 a public meeting was held at the Town Hall in Llantwit Major to consider such a proposal. Following this meeting, which was chaired by Dr J.W. Nichol-Carne of Dimlands, near Llantwit Major, Dr Nichol-Carne's nephew, Adam Blandy CE, prepared a survey of a route for an extension of the railway from Cowbridge to Llantwit Major. This was presented to a second public meeting, held at Cowbridge Town Hall on 2nd March, 1869, and presided over by Dr J.W. Nichol-Carne's brother and Mayor of Cowbridge, R. C. Nichol-Carne of Nash Manor, mid-way between Cowbridge and Llantwit Major. The proposed 'Llantwit Major Railway' was to run from Cowbridge station, passing via the valley of the River Thaw, to the south of the town, to a point just below St Mary Church, where it was to turn through nearly 90 degrees before running, via Llanmaes, to terminate in the Pound Field at Llantwit Major. The six miles of railway were to be laid out in the most economical manner at an estimated cost of only £30,000. A branch to serve Aberthaw could be added at a later date. Only a very limited service of two or three trains each way daily between Cowbridge and Llantwit Major was envisaged, but this was thought to be sufficient for the likely traffic.

A committee was formed to promote the construction of the Llantwit Major Railway, but it was not a good time for such schemes. The CR Co. was going through one of its periodic crises, and an economic recession had set in following the Overend Gurney Bank crash of 1866. As a result nothing came of the proposed Llantwit Major Railway.

Following the public meeting in Cowbridge in March 1869 an extended correspondence took place in the local press regarding the relative merits of Llantwit Major or Aberthaw as the terminus for an extension from Cowbridge. One such letter to the *Cardiff & Merthyr Guardian*, dated 12th March, 1869 and signed *'Ne sutor ultra crepidum'* (which loosely translated

means 'Don't talk about things you know nothing about' - which gives
something of the flavour of the exchange), ended by stating that:

> It is far more likely that instead of Cowbridge having the advantage of a continuation of
> the railway from that town to the sea, that a line will be carried 'coastways', passing
> through Llantwit Major and joining Barry and Bridgend . . . If ever a line was taken from
> Barry to Bridgend, all the traffic of the rich district along the coast would find its way
> via the Llynvi Railway to Aberdare, Hirwain and Merthyr.

Quite how use was to be made of the Llynvi Valley Railway is not at all clear
as this line then terminated just above Maesteg. Although a farmer named John
Thomas of Merthyr Dyfan, near Barry, had, in August 1861, put forward the
idea of a 'Glamorgan Coast Railroad' running from Pencoed to Penarth, via
Cowbridge and Barry, this reference by 'Ne sutor ultra crepidum' (whose identity
remains a mystery) provides the first known instance of a suggestion that a
railway should be built from Bridgend to Barry, via Llantwit Major.

At this date there was little at Barry, apart from a hamlet, for a railway to
serve. However, on 5th July, 1865 an Act had been obtained incorporating the
first Barry Railway Co., with powers to build railways from the SWR at
Peterston to Barry. The following year further Acts were obtained by this
company: on 11th June, 1866 Royal Assent was granted for the Barry Railway
(Alteration) Act, involving a new alignment for the line from Peterston to Barry;
and on 6th August, 1866 for the Barry Railway (Extension) Act for a branch
railway from Cadoxton to join the Penarth Railway at Cogan. Powers were also
obtained on 11th June, 1866 for the construction of a harbour at Barry.
Unfortunately, this was also the year of the Overend Gurney Bank crash and
ensuing financial panic. As a result this first Barry Railway scheme languished
through lack of support until it was abandoned by Board of Trade warrant on
5th August, 1874.

Nevertheless, it was from this source that there emerged the first concrete
proposal for a railway from Barry to Bridgend. On 11th March, 1870 two
engineers, Julian Tolmé and Richard Price-Williams, appeared before the TVR
Board of Directors seeking support for the promotion of such a railway. Tolmé
(1836-1878) was Engineer of the Barry Railway Co. from 1868 to 1871. Price-
Williams (1827-1916) was later Engineer to the ill-fated Ogmore Dock and
Railway scheme, and will appear again in our story. He was best known in
engineering circles for his pioneering work on the use of steel in permanent way
and for his statistical analysis of the life of permanent way and rolling stock.
Having listened to Tolmé and Price-Williams's proposition, the TVR Directors
declined to support the project. Nothing further was heard of this scheme until
29th May, 1871, when a writer to the *Cardiff & Merthyr Guardian*, signing himself
'A Landowner in the Vale', sought to reopen the debate on the best way to bring
railways to the Vale of Glamorgan. According to 'Landowner' the choice lay
between an extension of the Cowbridge Railway, or the adoption of Tolmé and
Price-Williams' scheme. His letter provides a clear indication that the route of
the latter proposal was to be via Llantwit Major, stating that: 'Either this line
(i.e. the CR) must be driven down to the sea or Messrs Tolmé and Price's [*sic*]

line must be adopted, in which case the town of Cowbridge will be shut out in the cold north as effectually as at present St Athans, Llantwit etc. are left destitute of railway accommodation'.

The following month the influential *Herapath's Journal*, read by railway speculators and promoters, reported that, 'Another effort is expected shortly to be made to open up the Vale of Glamorgan, either by an extension of the Cowbridge line to the coast or the construction of a railway from Bridgend to Barry'.

The article went on to note that the latter scheme was favoured by some of the principal landowners along its route. One such landowner was Dr J.W. Nichol-Carne of Dimlands. In the Nichol-Carne papers in the Glamorgan Archives is a contemporary sketch map showing a number of routes proposed for railways in the Vale, including the 'Bridgend and Barry Railway' of 1872. This line, which is believed to be that put forward by Tolmé and Price-Williams, differed from the later Vale of Glamorgan Railway in a number of significant ways. In particular, it was to follow a more southerly route between Bridgend and Llantwit Major, serving the villages of St Brides Major and Wick, *en route*. However, this early scheme was not taken any further, and with the abandonment of the original Barry Railway in 1874 an important incentive for building such a line disappeared.

Hopes for a railway extension southwards from Cowbridge also lingered on. In November 1872 the Great Western Railway published a notice for its Bill in the 1873 Session, which included application for powers to acquire the CR. Commenting on this development, *Herapath's Journal* speculated that, as it had always been the intention to continue this line to Aberthaw, takeover by the GWR was likely to bring about the early construction of such an extension. In the event, the GWR Act of 21st July, 1873 was confined to powers to enter into working and traffic agreements with the Cowbridge Co. Negotiations took place in 1874 with a view to the GWR taking over the working and management of the CR, but these proved fruitless, and so the local company was forced to struggle on until its increasingly decrepit undertaking was leased to the TVR in 1875.

With the failure of these early schemes the appetite for railway promotion in the Vale of Glamorgan appears to have faded away, the area reverting to its bucolic slumbers. These were to last undisturbed until the late 1880s.

Chapter Two

Promotion

Following the failure of the original Barry Railway scheme the 1870s saw off a number of attempts to promote railways to Barry, with the Penarth Sully and Cadoxton Railway (PS&CR) in the 1876 Parliamentary Session, the Penarth Sully and Barry Railway in 1877, and a revival of the Peterston-Barry scheme, also in 1877. Of these only the PS&CR came to anything, and then only in the truncated form of the Penarth Extension Railway, incorporated by Act of 11th August, 1876, and opened to passengers on 20th February, 1878. This period also saw mounting dissatisfaction with the accommodation provided for coal exports by the Bute Docks and the TVR, which led directly to the development of a proposal for a new dock at Barry, linked by an independent railway to the Rhondda coalfield. Various coal owners, prominent amongst them being David Davies of Llandinam ('Davies the Ocean'), John Cory, and Archibald Hood, with the support of the key landowner Lord Windsor, combined to promote the Barry Dock and Railway Bill in the 1883 Parliamentary Session. The Bill attracted widespread opposition from vested interests, surviving a 26-day passage through the Committee of the House of Commons, only to fall foul of the Lords Committee, which, on 26th July, 1883, found its preamble not proven.

Another Bill in the same Session proved more successful, at least as far as the Parliamentary hurdles were concerned. Promoted by pitowners in the Llynfi, Ogmore and Garw valleys, together with Bridgend businessmen, the Ogmore Dock and Railway (OD&R) Bill envisaged the construction of a new dock at the mouth of the River Ogmore, with a railway from there to join the South Wales main line of the GWR (just east of Bridgend station) and the Llynfi Valley line, north of its junction with that line. Plans for the dock were prepared by James Abernethy CE, with the railway being laid out by Richard Price-Williams. The latter gentleman, it will be recalled, had in 1870, together with fellow engineer Julian Tolmé, proposed the construction of a railway between Bridgend and Barry. Interestingly, the authorised railway was to have followed an almost identical route from Bridgend to Ewenny to that shown on the Nichol-Carne plan of the abortive Bridgend and Barry Railway of 1872.

The OD&R Act received Royal Assent on 20th August, 1883, but the presence of Tuskar Rock near the entrance to the proposed dock created uncertainty and the hoped-for support from the GWR failed to materialise. In November 1883 an attempt was made to interest the coal-owners of the Rhondda valleys in the Ogmore scheme when plans were deposited for the Pontypridd and Ogmore Railway (P&OR). Laid out by Richard Price-Williams, the P&OR was intended to provide a direct communication between the authorised OD&R north of Ewenny and the TVR at Pontypridd. This ambituous proposal was not taken any further, but an alternative route to Ogmore Dock for Rhondda coal could have been achieved had the GWR constructed railways between Hendreforgan, the Ely Valley and Porth, which had been authorised in 1882. However, the GWR showed no inclination to proceed with these lines, which had been put

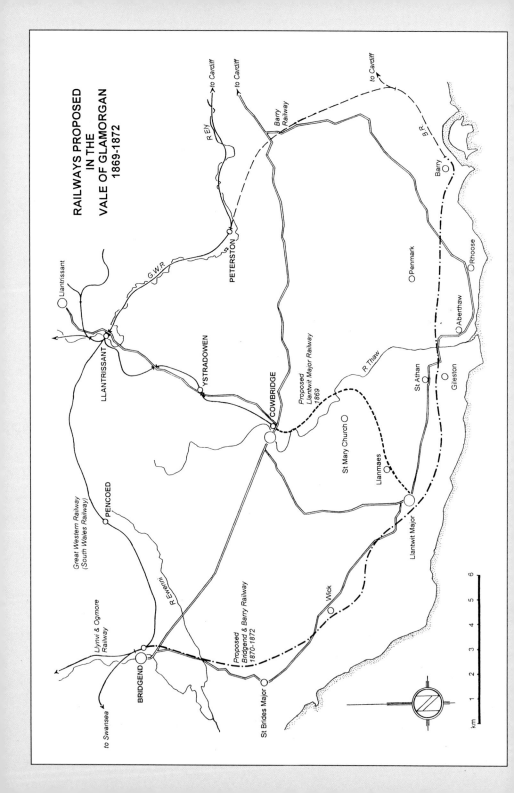

RAILWAYS PROPOSED
IN THE
VALE OF GLAMORGAN
1869-1872

forward as part of a scheme for a western outlet for Rhondda coal intended to counter the proposed Rhondda and Swansea Bay Railway (R&SBR), also authorised in 1882. In February 1886 the GWR refused a request from the Ogmore Dock & Railway promoters that it should enter into an agreement for working and maintaining their authorised railway and dock. Without such support the OD&R could not hope to proceed with the proposed works. An extension of time Act was obtained on 16th September, 1887, but without any liklehood of an early start to construction.

The Barry Dock promoters returned to the fray in the 1884 Session with a modified proposal designed to meet some of the objections of the previous year. These changes proved to be wise ones, as, despite continued opposition and a difficult passage though the Committees of the House, the Bill was passed and the Barry Dock and Railway (BD&R) Act received Royal Assent on 14th August, 1884. Unlike its Ogmore counterpart the incorporated company was able to raise the necessary capital, and on 14th November, 1884 the first sod of the new dock at Barry was cut, with due ceremony, by Lord Windsor. The first section of railway, between Cogan and Barry Dock, was opened to passengers on 20th December, 1888, and on 18th July, 1889 the official opening of the new dock took place. A branch railway connected the main line of the BD&R with that of the GWR at Peterston, thereby enabling coal from the Bridgend valleys to reach the new dock.

Thus by mid-1888 the future direction of railway development in the Vale of Glamorgan appeared to be relatively clear: the OD&R scheme, lacking the necessary support, was all but dead, despite its having obtained an extension of time Act in 1887; meanwhile, work was well advanced at Barry Dock and on its connecting railways, including the Peterston branch. Upon completion of these works a good outlet would become available for the coal of the Bridgend valleys, via the South Wales main line, the Peterston branch and the Barry main line.

However, in the middle of 1888 a new arrival in South Wales quickly changed this apparently settled prospect. In June 1888 Colonel John Thomas North (1842-1896) acquired the Llynvi & Tondu (L&T) Co., which owned coal mines and iron works to the north of Bridgend. An engineer from Leeds, North had made a fortune out of various nitrate entreprises in Chile, as a result of which he had acquired the sobriquet 'the Nitrate King'. He lived at Avery Hill, Eltham, where his neighbour was John Joseph Smith, receiver and manager of the L&T Co. This concern had been formed in 1880 following the reconstruction, by Smith, of the Llynvi Tondu & Ogmore Coal & Iron Co., which itself had originated in 1872 as a result of the merger of the Brogden empire and the Llynvi Iron Co. The new company fared no better than its predecessor, however, and in 1885 Smith was appointed as its receiver and manager. Following a number of unsuccessful attempts to sell the L&T Co., the property was put up for auction, by order of the Court of Chancery, on 11th January, 1887.

The story goes that it was at a garden party at Avery Hill that Smith and Colonel North concluded a deal whereby the latter was to acquire the L&T Co. North's bid for the company was formally accepted on 20th June, 1888, the

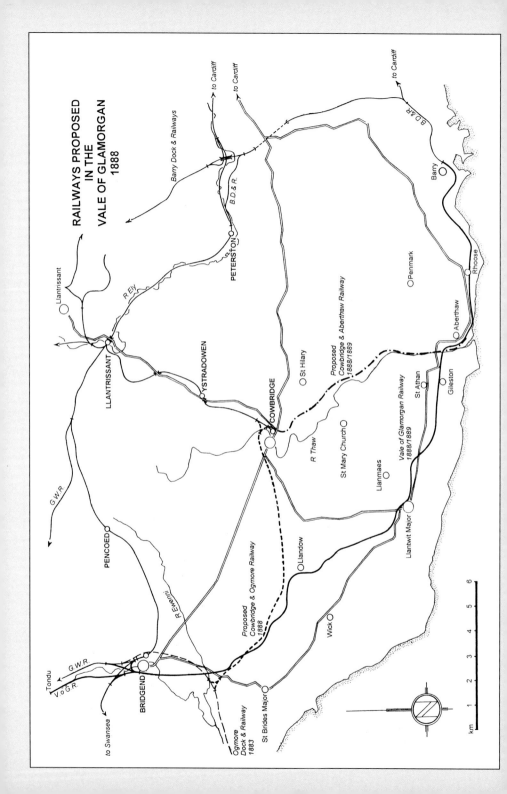

RAILWAYS PROPOSED
IN THE
VALE OF GLAMORGAN
1888

transaction being completed, on 10th July, 1888, through a private syndicate called the 'Western Navigation Collieries Syndicate'. Under a further agreement, dated 29th August, 1888, North undertook to transfer the contract of sale to this syndicate, which changed its name to 'North's Navigation Collieries Syndicate Ltd'. Finally on 19th January, 1889 this syndicate agreed to sell its assets to 'North's Navigation Collieries (1889) (NNC) Co. Ltd.', in which Colonel North was the major shareholder. The company had a registered capital of £450,000, divided into 90,000 shares of £5 each.

The property acquired by Colonel North comprised six collieries in the Bridgend valleys: Park Slip near Tondu; Wyndham and Tynewydd in the Ogmore Valley; and No. 9 Level, Maesteg Deep and Coegnant at Maesteg; together with iron works at Maesteg (which was rapidly dismantled and sold) and Tondu, and various other related assets. Extensive holdings of steam and house coal were also acquired, and a new pit was sunk at Caerau in the Llynfi Valley.

The collieries of NNC Co. were entirely dependent upon the GWR for the carriage of coal to the ports. The nearest outlet was Porthcawl, but this was hardly adequate for the needs of the export coal trade in the latter part of the 19th century. For such requirements the nearest ports were Cardiff and Penarth, and, when it opened, Barry, but these all involved lengthy journeys over GWR metals. The Cardiff and Ogmore Railway, opened in 1876 between Blackmill and Llanharan, together with the Tondu to Bryncethin Junction line, opened a year later, had shortened the distance from the Ogmore Valley and Tondu to Cardiff and Penarth, but at the expense of heavy gradients against the load. In addition, the GWR was about to provide a new curve at Brynmenyn and upgrade an existing connection at Tondu (both opened 21st November, 1892) to give direct runs from the Llynfi and Garw valleys onto the Cardiff and Ogmore line. However, in spite of these improvements, the coalowners of the Bridgend valleys, particularly Colonel North, felt that the GWR, with its monopoly position, was not giving their district as favourable treatment as appeared to be the case in other parts of South Wales. On the other hand, a dock at the mouth of the River Ogmore would be within much easier reach of the collieries of the Bridgend valleys. Initially it was to this prospect that Colonel North's attention was attracted, but another potential outlet for his traffic soon presented itself.

One of the Directors of NNC Co., Thomas Forster Brown CE, also acted as adviser to Colonel North. Forster Brown (1835-1907) had been born in Garrigill, Cumberland, and had made his entry to the South Wales mining and railway scene in 1858 when he was appointed Manager of Machen Colliery, near Caerphilly. In 1865 he was appointed Deputy Gaveller or Mineral Agent for the Crown in the Forest of Dean, a post he was to hold until 1903. At the end of 1866 Forster Brown went into partnership with Samual Dobson, the Engineer to the Penarth Harbour Dock and Railway Co., the firm being known as Dobson & Brown. Dobson died in 1870, his place in the partnership being taken by G.F. Adams. Adams was succeeded, on his death in 1884, by I.T. Rees, the firm then becoming Forster Brown & Rees. In addition to being responsible for the sinking of numerous collieries in South Wales, including that at Caerau for Colonel North, Forster Brown had also acted as engineer in the construction of a number of railways in the area. More importantly, he was, with John Wolfe Barry and Marc Brunel (son of I.K. Brunel), one of the engineers responsible for the construction of Barry Dock. In 1888 he was Chairman of the Monmouthshire & South Wales Coal Owners Association, and, on two occasions, served as President of the South Wales Institute of Engineers. With such a background Forster Brown was clearly an important and influential figure, being widely recognised as an authority on mining and railway matters in South Wales. His links with both Colonel North and the BD&R Co. were to be of crucial importance in the promotion of the Vale of Glamorgan Railway.

Forster Brown advised Colonel North that the GWR had only granted concessions elsewhere in South Wales under the threat of proposals for competitive lines. In particular, he cited the case of the Monmouthshire valleys and the withdrawal, in the 1888 Session, of the TVR's Bill for railways from Cardiff to those valleys in exchange for concessions from the GWR. In August 1888 Forster Brown, acting on behalf of NNC Co., met the GWR General Manager Henry Lambert, together with that company's Solicitor and two of its Directors, and sought a reduction in rates for coal carriage from the Bridgend valleys to Cardiff, Penarth and Barry. When the GWR failed to give satisfaction a scheme was developed for the 'Vale of Glamorgan Railway' (VoGR), linking the Bridgend valleys with Barry Dock. At this stage it is not at all clear whether this was a 'real' proposal or merely a 'paper' scheme designed to wring concessions from the GWR. Indeed, this latter interpretation is suggested by a comment made by Forster Brown, when before the House of Lords Committee on the VoGR Bill in the 1889 Session: 'I have no doubt that if Mr Lambert had met us (i.e. "given us satisfaction") at the time when we communicated with him, we should have thought no more about it'. On 15th October, 1888 Forster Brown wrote to Mr Lambert informing him of the intention to apply for an Act for the VoGR, but still the GWR remained non-commital.

Forster Brown's first thoughts for a railway from Bridgend to Barry involved a direct line, via Cowbridge, but in response to representations from interested parties in the Vale of Glamorgan, the proposed railway was rerouted via Llantwit Major. In his evidence before the House of Lords Committee on the VoGR Bill he confided that he, '. . . naturally felt, my clients felt too, that in promoting a railway of this kind the railway should be provided in the public interest. It is in the public interest that we propose the line in the direction it is now laid out'.

Acts of Parliament for the construction of railways granted the companies concerned special powers, including those for the compulsory purchase of property along the route, on the presumption that the railway would be of 'public and local advantage'. Reference to this was found in the preamble to the Act authorising the particular line. If such advantages were found to be lacking the preamble would be found 'not proven', and the Bill would be thrown out by the legislature. This provides the background to Forster Brown's remark about the 'public interest'. Whilst there would clearly have been advantages to a large part of the Vale of Glamorgan if the proposed line could be taken via Llantwit Major, this would have added about two miles to the journey for coal trains between the Bridgend valleys and Barry Dock, a very important consideration in such a competitive environment. Perhaps a more significant factor in this decision was the presence, in Cowbridge, of the TVR, and the emergence, in the autumn of 1888, of a proposal for the extension of the railway from that town to Aberthaw.

The idea of a railway from Cowbridge to Aberthaw had persisted despite the many difficulties faced by the CR Co., with pressure for such an extension continuing after the lease of the undertaking by the TVR in 1875. A line to Aberthaw could have provided an improved outlet for the agricultural produce of the Vale of Glamorgan, and would have encouraged the development of the lime industry of Aberthaw, but would have done little else. There was often wild talk of a dock at Aberthaw, but this was never to be a practical proposition. The prospects for the lime industry became more encouraging, however, when early in 1888 a company was formed to develop a lime works at Aberthaw. Clearly a railway connection would be of considerable advantage to such a scheme, and on 13th September, 1888 the TVR Board considered a request (dated 27th August, 1888) from the Aberthaw Lime Co. for an extension of the railway from Cowbridge to the works, then being built at Aberthaw. The Board was more favourably disposed to this suggestion than in earlier times, and the company's Engineer, H.O. Fisher, was instructed to prepare a survey of the route. A local company was promoted, with TVR support, to build the line, to be known as the 'Cowbridge and Aberthaw Railway' (C&AR). Evidence that the TVR also wished to safeguard its interests in the area to the south of Cowbridge is provided by a statement made by the TVR Chairman in May 1889, that there was no doubt about the C&AR being built, whether or not the TVR used it, but that it should be under TVR control. However, the role of any wider, more strategic considerations, such as an approach to Barry from the west or possible maritime development at Aberthaw, is far from clear.

It is likely that Forster Brown would soon have become aware of the activities of TVR surveyors south of Cowbridge, and also would probably have learned of that company's intentions through his many commercial contacts. A direct route for a railway from Bridgend to Barry, via Cowbridge, would have entailed the use of the Thaw Valley, south of Cowbridge, and undoubtedly this would have resulted in a confrontation with the TVR. At the same time, Parliament would not have looked with favour on the prospect of two competing lines in such close proximity. It is in this context that the case for routing the VoGR via Llantwit Major in the 'public interest' becomes much clearer: such a route would serve a different district to that of the C&AR scheme, thereby avoiding direct confrontation with the TVR and an uncertain and possibly damaging Parliamentary struggle.

In November 1888 plans were deposited and notices published for the C&AR and the VoGR. The former involved a simple extension from the Cowbridge Railway to the sea at Aberthaw, while the latter was to be on an altogether grander scale, with a total of five railways proposed to link the Tondu Ironworks (owned by NNC Co.) with Barry, with connections to the GWR at Bridgend. A route to the west of the centre of Bridgend was envisaged, with an independent station for that town and a tunnel under Newcastle Hill. At this stage the alternative route, involving an eastern approach to the GWR station, was still occupied, on paper at least, by the authorised Ogmore Dock & Railway. Running powers were sought over the BD&R from Barry to Cogan, over the Bridgend valleys lines of the GWR, and into that company's station at Bridgend. Also requested were powers to enter into working and traffic agreements with the GWR and the BD&R companies.

November 1888 also saw the deposition of plans for a third railway scheme in the Vale of Glamorgan. The Cowbridge and Ogmore Railway was to run from the CR, just north of Cowbridge station, to join the proposed OD&R line at Ewenny, with triangular junctions at each end of the line. The route of the proposed railway had been drawn up by Richard Price-Williams and a Mr Greathead. The involvement of the former indicates that the Cowbridge and Ogmore Railway was a creature of the OD&R promoters, designed as a cheaper, albeit more circuitous, substitute for the Pontypridd & Ogmore Railway scheme of 1883. Price-Williams's own estimate for coal traffic to Ogmore Dock, via the Cowbridge and Ogmore Railway, was relatively modest; he put it at only 150,000 tons per annum, out of an expected total for coal exports at the proposed dock, at its opening, of between 1,100,000 and 1,470,000 tons. The Cowbridge and Ogmore proposal may also have been a somewhat belated attempt to attract TVR support for the Ogmore Dock scheme. However, the TVR Minute Books are not helpful on this point, the only reference to the Cowbridge and Ogmore Railway being on 10th January, 1889, when a notice of intention to apply to Parliament for an Act for the railway was reported to the TVR Board. The date of this Minute suggests that the notice had been served on the TVR by the Cowbridge and Ogmore promoters, in connection with a proposed clause seeking powers to enter into working, traffic and other agreements with that company. Running powers over the CR were also to be sought. Despite superficial appearances to the contrary, it is most unlikely that it was envisaged that the Cowbridge and Ogmore Railway would be combined with the Cowbridge & Aberthaw Railway, at Cowbridge, to form an alternative route to that of the VoGR, between Bridgend and Aberthaw. The disposition of the proposed railways at Cowbridge was such that through running from the Cowbridge and Ogmore Railway onto the C&AR would not have been possible without major changes to the engineering parameters, of at least the former line, taking it outside the 'limits of deviation' shown on its deposited plans. The purpose of the chord lines at Cowbridge and Ewenny, shown on the Cowbridge and Ogmore plans, appears to have been to enable local trains to run direct between Cowbridge and Bridgend stations.

At this stage Colonel North still retained a foot in both the VoGR and the OD&R camps. Either he was undecided as to which would best serve his interests, or he was keeping his options open for as long as possible. Within days of the pubication of the notice for the VoGR Bill on 15th November, 1888, he became Deputy Chairman of the OD&R Co. At the same time it was announced that the Earl of Dunraven had consented to become Chairman of the Ogmore company, an event which prompted the *Cardiff Times* to assert that 'there is now every probability of this scheme being pushed forward with vigour'.

Forster Brown fought hard to convince Colonel North of the advantages of the VoGR, producing a strongly argued critique of the Ogmore proposals. Price-Williams countered with equal force, but eventually the Colonel came down in favour of the VoGR, and abandoned the Ogmore scheme to its fate. The Cowbridge and Ogmore Railway Bill was not proceeded with, and the dock proposal reverted to its former state of dormancy before being formally abandoned by an Act of 11th May, 1891. The precise point at which Colonel North reached this conclusion has not been established, and evidence of his reasoning is also lacking. However, as a hard-headed businessman he must have seen the hopelessness of the Ogmore proposals in the face of the strong support for the VoGR that was emerging from the BD&R Co. towards the end of 1888. In December of that year it was reported that the 'Barry people were throwing cold water' on the Ogmore scheme.

Doubts still remained as to the viability of the VoGR, however; writing on the subject on 12th February, 1889, George Downing, Secretary of the Barry Dock & Railway Co., expressed significant reservations on this point, and suggested that it might be as well to see what the GWR could offer in relation to traffic routed via Peterston Junction. Nevertheless, Downing appears to have been in a minority, as, on 15th February, 1889, the Barry Directors resolved to form a committee to negotiate with the VoGR promoters. Provisional agreement between the two parties was reached in April 1889, with the draft being approved by the Barry Board on the 16th of that month. Under the terms of the final agreement, dated 8th July, 1889, between the VoGR promoters (given as the NNC Co., R.R. Lockett, E.L. Evan-Thomas and R. Harvey) and the Barry Co., it was provided that:

> The VoGR Co. would complete a single line of railway, with works wide enough for a double line of rails, together with sidings at the junctions with the BD&R and the GWR.
> The BD&R Co. would work the new railway using its own rolling stock and staff, from the date of the completion of the line.
> The BD&R Co. would receive the gross receipts from working the railway, and would retain 60 per cent of this sum.
> If lower rates were to be charged via Peterston Junction for traffic from Bridgend to Barry Dock, the rates via the VoGR were to be reduced accordingly.

In addition, the agreement provided that the station houses were to be built of stone or brick, that the permanent way was to be of the BD&R Co.'s standard pattern, and that the number of intermediate stations was not to exceed six, unless otherwise agreed.

A relatively minor alteration was made to the route of the proposed railway before the VoGR Bill was considered in Parliament. On 11th April, 1889 a notice was published for a diversion of the line at Barry to enable it to run to the north of the Ship Hotel and make an end-on junction with the BD&R. This change allowed the Barry Co. to use land on the line of the old route for its own purposes.

The early part of 1889 saw the holding of a number of public meetings in support of the VoGR Bill. One such meeting took place at the Town Hall, Llantwit Major on 2nd January, 1889, when the proposal was warmly welcomed as one for which the inhabitants of the district had been wishing for 15 to 20 years. Referring to the intended design of Porthkerry viaduct, James Bell, Engineer to the BD&R Co., stated that it was envisaged that it would be of lattice girder construction, 'something like the Severn Bridge'. Fortunately, wiser counsels prevailed! Another meeting was held at the National School, Penmark on 11th March, 1889, when the proposed line was again welcomed enthusiastically.

Gestures of local support, although welcome, did little to ensure a smooth passage for the VoGR Bill through Parliament. The Bill came before the House of Lords Committee in June, and met opposition from a number of quarters. Somewhat surprisingly one of these was the BD&R Co., which opposed a clause in the Bill seeking running powers for the VoGR between Barry and Cogan, for the purpose of conveying coal to Penarth Dock. Always eager to obtain access to the territory of others, the BD&R was somewhat less willing to see potential traffic diverted elsewhere. Not wishing to cause further offence the VoGR promoters quickly withdrew this clause, and with it went Barry opposition. The Rhondda & Swansea Bay Railway claimed 'locus standi' (literally 'a place for standing', or a right to be heard) in view of its connection, at Cymmer, with the Llynfi and Ogmore section of the GWR, but this was rejected. Glamorgan County Council wished to see a clause inserted compelling the railway company to run passenger trains over the proposed railway. The County Council sought such clauses as a matter of policy, but its request was disallowed by the Committee. The OD&R petitioned against the Bill, but did not appear, having failed to persuade the GWR to provide financial support for its case. The most serious opposition came from the GWR itself on the grounds that it would suffer a loss of traffic to Barry, via Peterston Junction, but in spite of this the Bill was passed by the Committee. When the Bill came before the House of Commons Committee only the GWR opposed, this time with partial success as the Committee threw out the line from Tondu to Bridgend (Railway No. 4) and running powers north of Bridgend.

One further source of potential difficulty was removed when, on 15th July, 1889, an agreement was concluded between the VoGR promoters and the Cowbridge & Aberthaw Railway Co. concerning the demarcation between the two railways at Aberthaw. The C&AR Bill itself was unopposed, the company being incorporated by Act of 12th August, 1889.

The VoGR Act received Royal Assent on 26th August, 1889. The Act provided for the incorporation of the company with powers to build four lines of railway between Bridgend and Barry, and an authorised capital of £360,000 and powers to borrow up to £120,000. Three years were allowed for the compulsory purchase of land, and five years for the completion of the works. The GWR was required to 'punctually and regularly forward and afford all reasonable facilities' for goods and mineral traffic from its Llynfi and Ogmore section destined for Barry, and was to grant running powers to the VoGR for passenger and goods traffic into its Bridgend station. The Act also confirmed the agreement between the VoGR promoters and the BD&R Co., dated 8th July, 1889, already referred to.

The first Directors of the VoGR Co., as listed in the Act of 1889, were R. Harvey and E.L. Evans-Thomas, Directors of NNC Co., R.R. Lockett, a business associate of Colonel North, T.R. Thompson and E. Davies (son of David Davies), both Directors of the BD&R Co., A.F. Blandy CE, (who, it will be recalled, had in 1869 prepared plans for the abortive Llantwit Major Railway) and A. Drysdale, representing the Railway Share Trust Agency, which was to be charged with the disposal of the shares in the undertaking.

During the remaining part of 1889 detailed plans were drawn up, landowners contacted, and specifications prepared. On 25th October, 1889, in anticipation of a similar move by the TVR, the VoGR Board resolved to prepare a Parliamentary notice for a connection between the two lines at Aberthaw. The TVR did not come forward with such a scheme, however, and indeed nothing has been found to suggest that the company was even contemplating such a course of action. A notice was prepared by the VoGR for 'A Railway commencing by a junction with the Cowbridge and Aberthaw Railway, and terminating by a junction with Railway No. 1 authorised by the Vale of Glamorgan Railway Act 1889', but was not published. On 29th November, 1889 the *Barry & Cadoxton Journal* reported that the idea had been abandoned.

The following year started on an optimistic note. On 23rd January, 1890 the VoGR Board heard from their Engineer that the line had been staked out, that property plans and sections had been prepared, and that working drawings and specifications would be ready by the end of the month. At the company's first General Meeting on 20th February, 1890 hopes were expressed that the works would be commenced in early Spring. In March 1890 a tender for the construction of the railway was obtained from Lucas & Aird, but it was not until 7th May of that year that the Board resolved to seal an agreement with the contractors for the sum of £260,000, but only once all the authorised capital of the undertaking had been raised. The same meeting also saw the appointment of the key officers of the company, with Roderick Mackay as Secretary, Forster Brown and Rees as Engineers, J. Wolfe Barry as Consulting Engineer, and Blunt and Lawford as Solicitors.

A prospectus for the VoGR was issued in June 1890 when applications were invited for shares in the company. However, by 15th July, 1890 the amount applied for had reached only £171,000 out of the authorised capital of £360,000. Unsuccessful negotiations then took place with the contractors with a view to their taking shares in part payment, a sure sign of a scheme in trouble. To complicate matters certain large subscriptions were conditional upon the whole of the share capital being taken up. In these circumstances it was found necessary to return the applications for shares to the subscribers. Prospects for the undertaking were dealt a further blow in October 1890 following the Baring Bank panic and resulting financial crisis.

There were some faint signs of life in the early part of 1891. In January 1891 agents of an 'influential firm of contractors' were reported to be engaged on a survey of the route. In April the *Railway Times* noted that landowners along the route of the VoGR were being invited to take part of the purchase price of their land in shares, a further sign of the hopelessness of the situation.

Having seen off the threat of competition from the proposed Ogmore Dock, the Directors of the Barry Railway (ByR) Co. (as it had become by Act of 5th August, 1891) appear to have been reluctant to give further sustenance to the VoGR promoters in the wake of the share issue debacle of 1890, and the unsettled financial environment that followed. On 18th November, 1891 they declined to include any provision relating to the VoGR in the Barry Co.'s Parliamentary notice for the 1892 Session. However, the VoGR promoters were not prepared to let their scheme wither away, and, therefore, came forward with their own notice for the 1892 Session. Published on 18th November, 1891, this included the following provisions:

> Extension of time for the completion of the VoGR.
> Power to enter into working and traffic agreements with the GWR, TVR and C&AR companies.
> Transfer to and vesting in Barry Co. of VoGR.
> Authority for the Barry Co. to subscribe in and contribute funds towards the VoGR.
> Confirmation of a modified agreement with the Barry Co.
> Power to pay interest out of capital.

Although the ByR Board, taken as a whole, does not appear to have played any part in publishing this notice, at least two of its members were active in support of the VoGR. On 13th December, 1891 the VoGR Board approved the steps taken by NNC Co., in conjunction with Barry Directors, Messrs Thompson and Perks, in depositing the VoGR Bill for the 1892 Session. It appears, however, that neither the TVR nor the GWR had been consulted prior to the publication of the notice for the Bill. References to powers to enter into working and traffic agreements with these companies may, therefore, have been a negotiating ploy, designed to put pressure on the Barry Co. Reporting on this issue on 2nd January, 1892, Ammon Beasley, General Manager of the TVR, noted that as the powers sought were permissive they were not contrary to the interests of the company, and that no harm would result if they were not taken up.

The VoGR Bill was opposed by the GWR and ByR companies. The GWR contended that as the VoGR Co. was not in a financial condition to build the authorised railway, an extension of time should not be granted. The GWR's name had been included, without its consent, in the clause dealing with powers to enter into working and traffic agreements. In the case of the C&AR such powers could not be exercised because that company owned no rolling stock, while those relating to the TVR were unnecessary, uncalled for, and not in the public interest.

The ByR Co. opposed on the grounds that it was content with its existing agreement with the VoGR, and unwilling to alter it at the behest of that company. It also wished to see the deletion of references to working and traffic agreements with what it regarded, particularly in this context, as hostile companies. Although not specifically mentioned in the Bill, the VoGR promoters had in mind the provision of a junction with the C&AR, near Aberthaw. In their view, express powers for such a junction were not needed as the limits of deviation at Aberthaw, shown on the deposited plans of the two railways, were contiguous. Giving evidence before the House of Lords Committee on the VoGR Bill in May 1892, Forster Brown was of the view that this junction, if built, would provide the shortest route for traffic from the Ely and Treferig valleys and the Llantrisant and Llantwit Fardre districts, destined for Barry. The BD&R Act of 1884 had included powers for a junction between the Barry main line and the Llantrissant and Taff Vale Junction Railway at Creigiau, which would have provided a direct route to Barry from the areas mentioned by Forster Brown, but these had not been exercised. Now the ByR Co. feared that a junction at Aberthaw would be used to divert coal from the Rhondda valleys destined for Barry away from its own main line. Forster Brown thought that this was highly unlikely given the severe gradients and circuitous nature of the route via Llantrisant, Cowbridge and Aberthaw, but the ByR Co. could not be persuaded. Faced with such strong opposition from what should have been their natural ally, the VoGR promoters quickly relented and withdrew the offending clause and with it any talk of a junction with the C&AR at Aberthaw. The other clauses relating to the ByR were also withdrawn, and on 10th June, 1892 the somewhat diminished Bill passed unopposed through the House of Commons Committee. The resulting Act, which received Royal Assent on 20th June, 1892, was thus confined to an extension of time for the completion of the authorised railway and power to pay interest out of capital during its construction.

The Act of 1892 kept the VoGR alive, but it did not produce any immediate action to progress the scheme. However, elsewhere in the Vale things had not stood still since 1889. Construction of the C&AR had forged ahead, the first sod having been cut with due ceremony on 7th February, 1890, and by the middle of 1892 the works were nearing completion. On 20th July, 1892 a special train ran over the new line to Aberthaw Lime Works. On board were Ammon Beasley, General Manager of the TVR, Directors and officers of that company, the C&AR, and the Aberthaw Pebble Lime Co., Mr O.H. Jones of Fonmon Castle, Mr Mathias, the contractor, and, a reminder of the proximity of this new railhead to Barry, D.T. Alexander, President of the Barry Dock Chamber of Trade. We can only speculate about the nature of the 'several important matters' reported to have been discussed, but the only item made public was a decision (not acted upon) to build a 'jetty' across the mouth of the River Thaw to enable holidaymakers to pass from Aberthaw station to The Leys.

The C&AR was opened to passengers on 1st October, 1892. At the celebratory luncheon in Cowbridge, following the opening ceremony, a number of speakers referred to the possibility and desirability of extending the new line from Aberthaw to Barry. On 7th October, 1892 the *Barry Dock News* carried a report that land was being purchased along such a route by the C&AR Engineer, J.W. Brewer (who had succeeded H.O. Fisher as Engineer of the TVR), together with other unspecified gentlemen.

The opening of the C&AR, and the talk of its extension to Barry, appear to have concentrated the minds of the Barry Directors on the question of more positive support for the VoGR. If the VoGR was not proceeded with there was clearly a danger of the TVR stepping into the breach and promoting an extension of the C&AR to Barry. In such circumstances Parliament would not have needed much persuading to sanction such a line. In addition, there was a need to attract more coal traffic to the proposed second dock at Barry. The growth in the output of coal from the Bridgend valleys offered the prospect of increased tonnages for this dock, with a significantly greater share of revenue if it could be taken via the VoGR rather than via Peterston Junction.

The change in attitude towards the VoGR, which resulted from these considerations, was reflected in the powers sought in the ByR Bill in the 1893 Session of Parliament, the notice for which was published on 18th November, 1892. These included the transfer to and vesting in the ByR Co. of the powers for the construction of the VoGR, power to subscribe in and contribute towards the undertaking, and authority to lease the proposed railway. This notice anticipated the question of an arrangement between the two companies which was discussed by the Barry Directors on 2nd December, 1892. Having considered a report, prepared by the company's Solicitor, on the capital required by and the likely traffic of the VoGR, the Barry Directors informed Messrs Blunt and Forster Brown, representing the VoGR promoters, that they were prepared to insert a clause in their Bill to enable their company to guarantee the payment of interest or dividend on the VoGR Co. out of the share of the gross receipts retained by the ByR Co. This offer was dependent upon the two companies reaching an agreement whereby the Barry Co. would, in effect, assume full control over the VoGR. Negotiations were taken forward on this basis, and on 1st March, 1893 the Barry Directors were informed that the VoGR promoters 'might entertain' an arrangment guaranteeing them 4 per cent out of the 60 per cent of the gross traffic receipts to be retained by the Barry Co. This proved acceptable to both parties, and on 27th July, 1893 the ByR Directors approved the draft agreement.

The ByR Bill, then before Parliament, was modified to incorporate the principle underlying this proposed agreement, i.e. to permit the company to enter into and carry into effect agreements with the VoGR Co. concerning the apportionment of gross receipts. The resulting Act, which received Royal Assent on 24th August, 1893, also empowered the company to build its second dock at Barry.

With this proposed guarantee the prospects for an early start on the VoGR appeared to be more encouraging than at any time since the passing of its Act of Incorporation in 1889. However, there was a last minute hitch which could have put the entire project at risk. At a meeting of the Barry Directors on 27th February, 1894 reference was made to reports that NNC Co. and certain VoGR promoters were also actively engaged in the promotion of a rival scheme involving the creation of a modern dock at Port Talbot, with connecting railways to the Bridgend valleys. The old dock at Port Talbot had been owned, until his death in 1890, by Christopher Talbot, a Director of the GWR. Talbot had been unwilling to invest in the old dock and had not been prepared to see a railway built through the Duffryn Valley, linking Port Talbot with Maesteg.

He was succeeded by his eldest daughter, Emily Charlotte, who, through her agent Edward Knox, lost no time in trying to realise some of the value of her inheritance. An approach was first made to the GWR, seeking its assistance in the construction of a new dock at Port Talbot, together with the connecting railways. The GWR was prepared to back the latter, but not the former, which it considered would be unremunerative. In the face of this response, a syndicate was formed to take over the old dock and build the vital rail links. However, the GWR was not willing to abandon its claim to the Duffryn Valley, and so the 1894 Parliamentary Session witnessed a battle between the GWR proposals and the scheme for the Port Talbot Railway and Docks (PTR). The GWR Bill was thrown out, but that of the PTR proved more successful, receiving Royal Assent on 31st July, 1894. The new company's first Chairman was Lord Dunraven, but of greater significance to our story was the presence on the Board of Colonel John T. North, with Thomas Forster Brown listed as one of the Engineers. Work proceeded rapidly on the new undertaking, with the dock opening in 1898 and the railways in 1897 and 1898.

But to return to February 1894: the involvement of NNC Co. and Forster Brown in the promotion of the Port Talbot scheme appears to have come as something of a surprise to the Barry Directors, who threatened not to proceed with the proposed agreement with the VoGR Co. However, Colonel North's strong association with the emerging Port Talbot proposals did not prevent him from, once again, keeping his feet firmly planted in two opposing camps. He was clearly reluctant to see the Barry guarantee for the VoGR fall by the wayside. On 14th March, 1894 the Barry Directors decided that, as a result of assurances given by Colonel North and others, there was no longer any objection to the guarantee agreement being sealed. This agreement, entered into between the VoGR promoters, NNC Co., and the ByR Co., was dated 28th May, 1894. On the same day a separate agreement was made between North's company and the two railway companies whereby NNC Co. undertook to send 360,000 tons of coal each year for 20 years to Barry Docks, via the VoGR. Under a further agreement, dated 3rd December, 1894, the Ocean Coal Co. pledged half of its output of large steam coal from the Garw Valley to the VoGR route.

With this final difficulty resolved to the satisfaction of the Barry Board, the VoGR Co. published its second prospectus on 29th June, 1894. The dominant infuence of the Barry Co. was readily apparent, with no less than six of the seven VoGR Directors listed in the prospectus also being members of the Barry Board; the seventh, E.L. Evans-Thomas represented NNC Co. The Barry Directors were Archibald Hood, Edward Davies, John Cory, Robert Forrest, Thomas Thompson and Frederick Davis. The Engineers were Forster Brown and Rees and James Szlumper (1834-1926), with John Wolfe Barry (1836-1918) as Consulting Engineer. Both Szlumper and Barry were knighted in 1894. The Solicitors were Downing and Handcock of Cardiff, and the Secretary was W. Mein, who also acted as Secretary to the Barry Co.

With the exceptionally strong backing provided by the Barry guarantee there was no difficulty in attracting applications for the whole of the share capital, and on 12th July, 1894 the VoGR Board resolved to invite tenders for the construction of the works. On 8th August, 1894 the Engineers of the two railway companies inspected the ground at Barry, and two days later the tender of Pethick Bros., for the sum of £182,444, was accepted for the construction of the section of the line between Barry and Ewenny.

The List will open on the 3rd day of July, 1894, and be closed on or before the 5th day of July, 1894.

Section 7 of the Vale of Glamorgan Railway Act 1892 authorises the payment of interest out of capital.

Vale of Glamorgan Railway Company.

AUTHORISED SHARE CAPITAL - - - £360,000

In 36,000 Shares of £10 each, of which 12,000 Shares have already been applied for by the Directors.

Borrowing Powers - - - - £120,000

ISSUE OF 36,000 SHARES OF £10 EACH.

A new and direct route from the Llynvi, Garw, and Ogmore Coalfields to Barry Dock.

TO BE WORKED BY THE BARRY RAILWAY COMPANY IN PERPETUITY AT A FIXED PERCENTAGE OF GROSS RECEIPTS, THE BARRY COMPANY'S PROPORTION OF SUCH RECEIPTS IN EACH YEAR TO BE APPLIED, IF NECESSARY, IN THE PAYMENT OF FOUR PER CENT. UPON THE ORDINARY CAPITAL OF THE COMPANY.

THE SHARES WILL BE PAYABLE AS FOLLOWS :—

Ten Shillings on application, £1 on allotment, 10s. on the 1st day of October, 1894, and the Balance in calls not exceeding £2 per Share at intervals of not less than three months.

Under the powers of the Company's Act of 1892, Section 7, and in accordance with the terms thereof, interest at the rate of 3 per cent. per annum upon the amount from time to time paid up (not exceeding £24,000 in the whole) will be paid during the time limited for construction.

Subscribers paying in advance of calls will be entitled to interest at the rate of three per cent. per annum upon the amount paid in advance.

Directors.

ARCHIBALD HOOD, Cardiff, Deputy Chairman Barry Railway Company, and Managing Director Glamorgan Coal Company, Limited, *Chairman.*

EDWARD DAVIES, Llandinam, Montgomeryshire, Director Barry Railway Company, and Chairman of the Ocean Coal Company, Limited, *Deputy Chairman.*

JOHN CORY, (Messrs. Cory Brothers & Co., Limited, Cardiff), Director Barry Railway Company.

ROBERT FORREST, Saint Fagans, Director Barry Railway Company.

THOMAS ROE THOMPSON, Cardiff, Director Barry Railway Company, Shipowner and Colliery Proprietor.

FRED. L. DAVIS, Ferndale, South Wales, Director Barry Railway Company, and Chairman D. Davis & Sons, Limited.

E. L. EVAN-THOMAS, Gnoll, Neath, and Dock House, Billiter Street, London, Director North's Navigation Collieries 1889, Limited.

Bankers.

THE METROPOLITAN BANK OF ENGLAND AND WALES, LIMITED, Barry Dock.

Consulting Engineer.

J. WOLFE BARRY, Delahay Street, Westminster.

Engineers.

FORSTER BROWN AND REES, Cardiff.

J. W. SZLUMPER, C.E., 17, Victoria Street, Westminster.

Solicitors.

DOWNING AND HANDCOCK, Cardiff.

Secretary and Offices.

W. MEIN, Barry Dock.

Vale of Glamorgan Railway Prospectus, 29th June, 1894.

2

PROSPECTUS.

This Company has been incorporated by special Act of Parliament for the purpose of constructing the Railway (coloured red on the enclosed map) from Bridgend to Barry Dock, thereby providing a new and direct access from the Llynvi, Garw, and Ogmore coal district to the Dock at Barry.

The Vale of Glamorgan Railway will, when constructed, be worked in perpetuity by the Barry Railway Company under an Agreement scheduled to the Company's Act. This Agreement comes into operation immediately upon the completion of the Railway, and provides that the Barry Company shall maintain, manage, man, stock and work the Railway, paying rates and taxes and other outgoings. The Barry Company will, in consideration of these services, be entitled to 60 per cent. of the gross receipts after certain deductions are made, but this sum is to cover the cost of working the traffic of the Glamorgan Railway over the Dock Railways and Sidings of the Barry Company up to the Tips and Quays in and round Barry Dock. The 60 per cent. payable to the Barry Company is applicable in each year to pay the shareholders of this Company 4 per cent. upon the ordinary capital, in case the receipts of this Company prove insufficient, so that the whole of the gross receipts of each year (excepting this Company's cost of offices, staff, management expenses, and payments to be made by the Company under the terms of the agreement) will be available for that dividend ; but it is confidently anticipated that the dividend arising from the net receipts of this Company will exceed 4 per cent. per annum.

Protection and facilities for the due and proper forwarding of traffic to and from the Llynvi, Garw, Ogmore, and Avan Valleys have been secured by clauses inserted in the Vale of Glamorgan Railway Act requiring the Great Western Company to punctually and regularly forward and afford all reasonable facilities for goods and mineral traffic destined for or coming from those valleys, viâ the Vale of Glamorgan Railway, at rates per mile not greater than their own lowest rate for like traffic between the same places and the Docks at Cardiff, Penarth, or Barry, with contingent running powers over the railways of the Great Western Company in the Llynvi, Garw, Ogmore, and Avan Valleys in case of the Great Western Railway Company failing to comply with the Act. Provision is also made by the Act for the due accommodation of the Vale of Glamorgan traffic at the Great Western Railway Company's Bridgend Station.

The Company have entered into contracts, mostly based upon output, with owners of collieries guaranteeing to the Vale of Glamorgan Railway a mineral traffic, which, together with the arrangement entered into with the Barry Company, in the opinion of the Directors make the present issue of capital a most desirable investment.

The Directors have already subscribed for a third of the capital, £120,000,which is the largest amount they can subscribe under the regulations of the Stock Exchange.

In addition to the export mineral traffic, the import traffic in pit wood, iron ore, and general merchandise in connection with the collieries and iron works is expected to be very considerable. The line, which is twenty miles in length and extends from the town of Bridgend to Barry, passes through a rich agricultural district, and now that the Barry Company exercises its running powers into Cardiff, will become the main line between Cardiff and the Vale of Glamorgan.

The local traffic also promises to be important.

The population of the Barry district alone, which in 1884, when the Barry undertaking was authorised, did not exceed 1,000, is now about 15,000. Means of communication by railway between Cardiff, Barry, and the Vale of Glamorgan are greatly needed, and the Directors feel confident that a considerable passenger traffic will be carried on the railway of the Company.

Vale of Glamorgan Railway Prospectus, 29th June, 1894.

3

The coalfield with which the Vale of Glamorgan Railway communicates is reported by Mr. Forster Brown to—

"contain upwards of 1,500 million tons of coal, and, therefore, more coal than the Rhondda Valley district, out of which, at the present time, between 7,000,000 and 8,000,000 tons of coal are produced annually, chiefly for export. The district being further away from a good port has not as yet been developed to the same extent as the Rhondda Valley district; and until within the last few years the upper bituminous seams of this district were chiefly worked for ironworks and local purposes. Latterly, however, the steam coals which lie deeper have begun to be developed, and the outputs last year were about 2,000,000 tons, showing an increase in output of over 60 per cent. in the last seven years; whilst further large developments are in progress, comprising two new pits in the Avan Valley, three new steam coal openings upon North's Navigation property, approaching completion, and a new steam coal Colliery at Garth, and when the new developments which are now in progress are completed the output of steam coal will be increased by upwards of three-fourths of a million tons per annum ; and practically the whole of this increase will require to be exported. After a further period of years the output will probably be increased by about another two million tons a year, bringing up the ultimate approximate estimated output to about five million tons per annum."

The importance of Barry as a place of shipment for Welsh coal has been fully established by the results of the first five years of the Barry Railway Company's working. Coal is now being shipped at the rate of between 4½ and 5 million tons per annum.

The Barry Dock is 73 acres in extent with deep water, and its existing value will shortly be much enhanced by the Deep Water Lock which has been constructed and is rapidly approaching completion. This Lock will enable vessels to enter and leave the Dock at all states of tide, and will thus afford facilities for despatch which are not possessed by any other Dock in the Bristol Channel.

The Barry Railway Company have invited tenders for the construction of a new Dock, and it is believed, with the additional accommodation and facilities afforded, the trade will be largely increased.

It is well known that the railways in South Wales, which derive their principal traffic from minerals, are among the best dividend-paying lines in the country. The Barry 4 per cent. preference shares, with which this issue will bear favourable comparison, now stand at over twenty per cent. premium.

The amount from time to time paid up during the construction of the line will bear interest payable out of capital at the rate of 3 per cent. per annum during the period limited by the Act for the construction of the railway, and not exceeding in the whole the sum of £24,000.

The Directors are advised that the line, which presents no engineering difficulties, can be completed and opened for traffic in about two years.

Application for Shares should be made on the enclosed form, accompanied by a payment of Ten Shillings per Share on the number of Shares applied for, and forwarded to the Metropolitan Bank of England and Wales, Limited, Barry Dock, or any of the branches thereof.

Application will be made to the Stock Exchange for an official quotation.

The Acts of Parliament, Working and other Agreements may be inspected at the Office of the Company's Solicitors, Vienna Chambers, Cardiff. Prospectuses may be obtained from the Bankers at their various branches, and from the Solicitors and Secretary.

29th June, 1894.

Vale of Glamorgan Railway Prospectus, 29th June, 1894.

Chapter Three

Construction and Inspection

A formal commemoration of the start of work on the VoGR, involving the customary cutting of the first sod, was arranged for Monday 20th August, 1894, nearly five years to the day after the passing of the company's Act of Incorporation. The ceremony took place in a field near Harbour Road, Barry, and was performed by Mrs W. Szlumper, wife of the Resident Engineer, William Szlumper, who was also in attendance. Also present were Thomas Forster Brown, F. Brown, the contractor's agent, and F.T. Rendall, Sub Engineer. Having completed the necessary exertions, the party adjourned to the nearby Ship Hotel to partake of the equally customary luncheon.

The second week of September 1894 saw members of the engineering staff engaged in pegging out the route of the new railway. Preparations also took place at each end of the line, with storehouses, offices and other facilities being erected. Navvy camps were established at various points between Barry and Bridgend. On 10th September, 1894 preparatory work started at the site of Porthkerry viaduct, the major structure on the VoGR.

At this point it will be appropriate to pause and examine a number of important changes which had been made, or were in the course of being made, to the plans for the new railway.

On 17th August, 1894 the ByR Co. had obtained an Act authorising the construction of a railway from Barry station to Barry Island for the purpose of developing the already significant tourist traffic to the 'Island'. The 'Barry Island Railway' was to form a junction just to the east of the end-on junction between the Barry line and the VoGR.

It will be recalled that the route of the railway at Bridgend, as authorised by the VoGR Act 1889, passed to the west of the town and involved a complex set of junctions with the South Wales main line and the Llynfi Valley branch to the west of the GWR station. The formal abandonment of the OD&R scheme in 1891 opened the way for a simpler and cheaper route to the east of the town, with a short spur joining the South Wales main line, just before Bridgend station, and a loop line for mineral traffic continuing to join the Llynfi Valley branch about 1 mile to the north of that station. Under this arrangement an independent station for the VoGR in Bridgend was not necessary. On 27th February, 1894 the ByR Engineer, James Bell, submitted a plan of this 'Deviation Line' to his Directors. In addition to the various practical advantages, this route would be about £40,000 cheaper than the authorised one, representing a significant reduction in the overall cost of the railway. The Deviation Line proposal was approved, and in November 1894 plans for the line were deposited for the 1895 Session of Parliament. The Act itself received Royal Assent on 20th June, 1895, but the Deviation Line had already been staked out, and on 5th July, 1895 the VoGR Board accepted Pethick Bros' offer of £45,000 for its construction. The Act also provided for the abandonment of the original route north of Ewenny and for a further extension of time, of three years, for

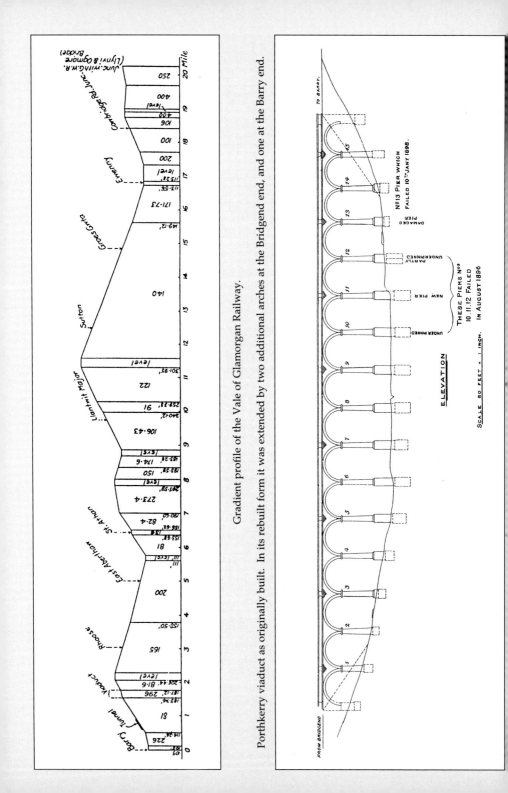

Gradient profile of the Vale of Glamorgan Railway.

Porthkerry viaduct as originally built. In its rebuilt form it was extended by two additional arches at the Bridgend end, and one at the Barry end.

completion of the remainder of the works originally authorised in 1889. The third major change came about in stages. The agreement made between the VoGR promoters and the ByR Co. in July 1889 had envisaged the provision of a single line of rails over the whole of the new railway, with passing loops at stations. There appears to have been a gradual realisation that this would not be an efficient way of handling the likely volume of traffic. In August 1894 it was arranged to make Porthkerry tunnel wide enough for double track, at an additional cost of £10,000. On 5th October, 1894 the VoGR Board resolved to form the line for double track throughout, and to lay a double line of rails between Barry and Rhoose. Finally, on 7th June, 1895 it was agreed to lay a double line all the way from Barry to Bridgend, including the Coity loop line. Authority to raise the additional capital required to accommodate this change in plan was obtained in the VoGR Act of 1895.

The fourth and final change was of a more minor nature. On 5th July, 1895 the VoGR Board approved a proposal whereby the junction with the GWR at Coity would be moved 500 yds to the north to enable the total length of the nearby exchange sidings to be doubled to five miles. Although minor, this change still required Parliamentary authority, which was provided by the VoGR Act of 15th July, 1897.

Work on the new railway got off to a somewhat ominous start: the excavations for the foundations of Porthkerry viaduct uncovered 'bad ground', which necessitated going deeper than had been anticipated. It would be wrong to suppose that, on a project of this scale, construction started at one end of the line and proceeded, in a more or less orderly fashion, to the other. In fact during the first month work commenced in no less than 25 cuttings along the route. Balancing cut and fill was of central concern to the Engineers, and stone for masonry was to be obtained from sources along the line. The opening up of these cuttings, therefore, provided the essential resources for the construction of bridges and embankments. Work also started on the other major work of the undertaking, Porthkerry tunnel, where, by the end of October 1894, the heading at the Bridgend end had been driven some 35 yards.

November 1894 saw the start of what was to be a recurring problem throughout the construction of the VoGR. Bad weather, which caused considerable delay to the works during the month, was to continue through December and into the early part of 1895. Taking advantage of the resulting hiatus, tunnelling was commenced from the Barry end of Porthkerry tunnel, and by the end of January 1895 a total of over 200 yds of the tunnel had been dug.

The weather improved in March 1895, and the resulting increase in the rate of work was reflected in the number of men employed, which rose to nearly 1,000 during the month. Substantial quantities of earthwork and masonry were completed during this and the following months. On 23rd April, 1895 the headings at Porthkerry tunnel were taken through, and lining out commenced. During May a start was made on the short tunnel (Porthkerry No. 2), near Porthkerry church.

Good progress was maintained during the summer and autumn of 1895, with about four-fifths of the viaduct completed, 266 yds of tunnel lined out, and 16 bridges constructed by the end of November. However, once again the onset of

Porthkerry viaduct following the partial collapse during construction on 18th August, 1896.

Lens of Sutton

An Edwardian view of Porthkerry viaduct.   *Author's Collection*

bad weather during the winter months led to a substantial slowdown in the rate of work. Nevertheless, the Engineers remained confident that the line would be completed on time. The railway was certainly taking shape; during December nearly 600 yds of permanent way were laid.

In the early part of March 1896 a serious slippage occurred in the large embankment where the railway crossed the Thaw Valley, to the west of Aberthaw. This slip, amounting to about 20 ft, was the third at this spot and brought the total slippage here to about 50 ft. The difficult ground conditions in the valley were not helped by the 'wet and rough' weather which continued through March.

Despite apparent progress with the works concern began to mount that the railway would not be completed by 26th August, 1896, as provided for in the contract for its construction. On 10th April, 1896 the VoGR Board instructed its Solicitor to write to the contractor reminding him of the consequences of failing to complete the work by the date specified in the contract. After this warning shot the work rate picked up somewhat. To speed things up night work was introduced wherever, as the Engineers' report put it, 'the men can be induced to work'. A further improvement took place in May 1896, but night work in the cuttings west of Porthkerry and near Aberthaw had to be suspended following an objection on grounds of danger to shipping from the Elder Brethren of Trinity House, under the provisions of the Merchant Shipping Act of 1894, an Act of which the Engineers had not previously been aware. The number of men employed on the works reached a peak of 2,200 at this time.

This improvement was destined not to last, however, and in June 1896 the rate of work declined significantly, although on a more positive note Porthkerry viaduct was nearing completion and the nearby tunnel had been lined throughout. As a result of this slowdown the contractor, Mr Pethick, was summoned before the VoGR Board on 3rd July, 1896, and taken to task for his unsatisfactory performance. Once again this appears to have had the desired effect, with the July returns showing a significant improvement. By the end of that month all bridges on Contract No. 1 (Barry to Ewenny) had been completed, the arches of Porthkerry viaduct were all in place, and at the nearby tunnel only the masonry faces of the portals remained to be done.

Work on the viaduct appeared to be progressing satisfactorily when, on 18th August, 1896, disaster struck. Pier No. 10, the sixth from the Barry end, began to show signs of settlement and started to subside. Two days later pier No. 11 failed in the same way. Sir James Szlumper hastened to the scene, and, on 22nd August, produced a report in which he described this failure, in something of an understatement, as 'very unfortunate and most annoying'. According to Sir James, the excavations for the stricken piers had been taken down to what appeared to be solid rock - 'splendid foundations' in his words - but it was now clear that this rock overlay clay, and that this had led to the subsidence of the piers when the final weight of the arches was applied. To remedy this situation it was necessary to dismantle pier No. 11, remove its foundations, and take the excavation down a further 18 ft 9 in. Pier No. 10 was underpinned and the three adjoining arches rebuilt. Apart from seriously delaying the completion of the railway, the failure of these piers gave an indication of a potentially serious deficiency which was to manifest itself later on with even more disastrous results. Wet weather returned in October 1896 to compound the delay to the works. Things improved during the following month, but there still remained a fair amount of work to be done, especially in the cuttings. By the end of the year about three-quarters of the permanent way had been laid, but a significant amount of bridge work remained unfinished on the Deviation Line. Once again a wet winter did not help, but things improved sufficiently during the Spring for Sir James Szlumper to state, at the VoGR Board on 6th May, 1897, that the contractor had indicated that he expected the works to be completed by the end of June. Unfortunately, this proved over-optimistic as progress fell well short of expectations. Various items remained to be completed, but in the end it was the remedial work on Porthkerry viaduct which was to determine the completion date for the new railway. It was not until 1st October, 1897 that this work was finished.

When work had started on the VoGR in 1894 there were firm plans for only four stations: Southerndown Road; Llantwit Major; Gileston/St Athan (the name Gileston was not fixed until near the end of 1896); and Aberthaw. In October 1894 the Engineers recommended additional stations at Rhoose and Fontigary, but only the former was proceeded with. Plans of the station yards at Aberthaw and 'St Athan' were approved on 5th July, 1895, with those at Rhoose and Southerndown Road being settled during September. The layout at Llantwit Major was subject to further consideration, however, it being found necessary, where the line crossed the Llanmaes Road, to provide a bridge wide enough for three lines of rails in order obtain a workable arrangement.

The station buildings were to prove more contentious. On 3rd February, 1896 the Engineers reported that a plan had been prepared for buildings at Aberthaw station modelled on those at Wenvoe on the ByR main line, where the somewhat belated introduction of a passenger service was due to take place on 16th March, 1896. No decision was reached at the time, but at the beginning of March, with the platform walls under construction at Aberthaw, the Engineers pressed for further instructions on this point. The Wenvoe design was clearly felt to be over-elaborate - and no doubt too expensive - for the VoGR, as on 6th March, 1896 the Board ordered fresh plans to be prepared. These, to a somewhat simpler design, were approved by the VoGR Board on 10th April, 1896. At the same meeting instructions were given to obtain six signal boxes from Evans O'Donell & Co. for the sum of £820 18s. It was originally intended that there would be not be any level crossings on the line, but during the building of Rhoose station it became apparent that it would be advantageous to provide such a crossing to the east of the station controlled by the station signal box. This arrangement was approved by the Board on 3rd June, 1896. Work on the station buildings at Aberthaw commenced in June 1896, and on 3rd September, 1896, the tender of Jenkins & Sons was accepted for the construction of similar buildings on the rest of the line. Footbridges at the stations were supplied by Lysaght & Co., the tender being accepted on 30th December, 1896.

At Bridgend VoGR passenger and goods trains were to make use of the GWR station, running powers being granted by agreement dated 10th January, 1896. Although the GWR quickly came up with a plan of the accommodation

Efail Isaf station on the Cadoxton-Trehafod line of the Barry Railway, 15th July, 1953. Drawings to this design were prepared for the Vale of Glamorgan Railway stations, but rejected in favour of something simpler and cheaper.   *R.M. Casserley*

proposed for the VoGR little else happened, and on 6th March, 1896 the VoGR Board determined, with evident frustration, to complete their line up to the GWR boundary. It was not until the following October that agreement was reached on the arrangements to be provided at the station. The junction itself was put in during May 1897. Vale passenger trains were provided with a bay platform on the down side of the station.

A new railway had to be inspected by an Inspector appointed by the Board of Trade and approved before passenger trains could be run. There were a number of inspections of different parts of the VoGR, but all were undertaken by Lt Colonel H.A. Yorke RE, who later became Chief Inspecting Officer at the Railway Inspectorate. Lt Colonel Yorke's first report was dated 2nd August, 1896 and dealt with the junction of the Barry Island Railway at Barry. At this stage the connection to the VoGR took the form of a simple double junction, with both lines of the VoGR fitted with trap points to guard against runaways.

At the other end of the line application was made by the GWR in September 1896 for Board of Trade sanction for the arrangements at Coity Junction. Having been assured that these were of a temporary nature, pending completion of the doubling of the line between Bridgend and Tondu, the Board of Trade agreed to grant provisional sanction for the junction. The new works were notified as complete and ready for inspection on 25th October, 1896. They were inspected by Lt Colonel Yorke, who completed his report on 4th January,

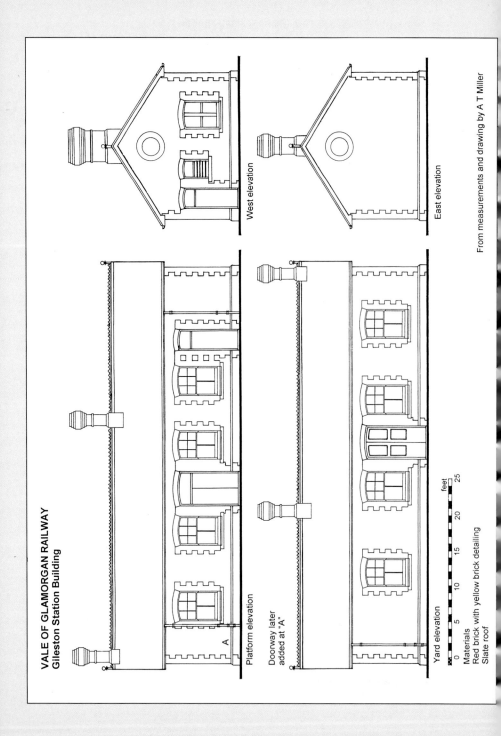

VALE OF GLAMORGAN RAILWAY
Gileston Station Building

Platform elevation

Doorway later
added at "A"

A

West elevation

Yard elevation

East elevation

Materials
Red brick with yellow brick detailing
Slate roof

feet
0 5 10 15 20 25

From measurements and drawing by A T Miller

1897. Yorke recommended that approval be given for the junction, which was controlled by a new two-lever ground frame. This was subsequently replaced by a brick-built signal box containing 35 levers. The junction itself was brought into use for construction traffic during May 1897.

On the main line of the VoGR the necessary first notice was submitted to the Board of Trade on 24th August, 1897, indicating that it was intended to open the railway 'after the expiration of one calender month from this date'. It was not until 9th October, 1897, however, that the second notice was forwarded, stating that the line would be ready for inspection at any time during the 10 days after 11th October, 1897. Lt Colonel Yorke made a preliminary inspection of Porthkerry viaduct on 14th and 15th October 1897. Three days later he completed a favourable report on the new junction with the GWR at its Bridgend station. He returned to make a further inspection of Porthkerry viaduct on 6th November, 1897, and, four days later, he completed a full report on the VoGR. His report stated:

I have the honour to report for the information of the Board of Trade, that in compliance with the instructions contained in your Minute of the 11th October, I have inspected the Vale of Glamorgan Railway.

This commences at its junction with the Barry Railway at Barry station, and terminates, so far as passenger traffic is concerned, at Bridgend station on the GWR.

The line is double throughout except at three of the stations where four lines of rails have been laid, the gauge is 4 ft 8½ in. and the length is 18 miles 60 chains.

The steepest gradient has an inclination of 1 in 81, and the sharpest curve a radius of 15 chains.

The cuttings and embankments are numerous and of considerable magnitude; some of the former have depths of 58, 51, 50 and 49 ft, while the principal embankments vary in height from 47 ft to 28 ft. Some of the embankments will require careful watching for some time to come.

The permanent way is laid with steel rails weighing 82 lbs per yd, chairs of 41 lbs each, and creosoted sleepers of the usual dimensions. The line is well ballasted with broken limestone and is in good order.

There are 17 bridges over and 29 under the line. Five of the former and 10 of the latter have wrought iron girders resting upon masonry abutments, the spans being for the most parts 25 ft and in no case exceeding 35 ft. The girders have sufficient theoretical strength, and the deflections of those under the line when tested with the heaviest engines available were moderate.

The other bridges are constructed with brick arches either semi-circular or segmental, and masonry abutments.

There is one large viaduct having 16 openings 13 of which have arched spans of 50 ft and three of 45 ft each. The arches are semi-circular and are composed of six rings of brickwork laid in lias lime mortar, while the piers are constructed with stone masonry facings hearted with cement concrete. The maximum height of this viaduct to rail level is 110 ft and several of the piers are 76 ft high.

When the centres of the arches of this structure were first struck, two of the piers, viz: the fifth and sixth from the east end sunk 4 ft owing to failure of the foundations. One of these piers was subsequently dismantled and reconstructed, while the other was under-pinned to a depth of 26 ft. The three arches adjacent to these piers were also dismantled and rebuilt.

The viaduct is a handsome work, but its design presents several features which are open to criticism.

The arches are very light, and should according to modern practice possess at least seven rings of brickwork in place of six; the bricks should have been laid in cement in place of lime mortar; the piers would have been stronger if built of coursed masonry throughout in place of being 'hearted' with concrete, the absence of any block piers (or abutment piers) in a work of this magnitude is a source of weakness; and lastly the load on the foundations, which amounts to over 7 tons per sq. ft is excessive.

The difficulties already alluded to, which occurred during the construction of this viaduct owing to the failure of some of the foundations, and the fact that one pier has been underpinned to so great a depth as 26 ft, combined with the features of the general design which I have just enumerated render it impossible for me at present to express a favourable opinion of this structure.

I first inspected the viaduct on October 14th, and I made a further inspection of it on November 6th. Between these dates the Engineers of the Company have at my suggestion caused the heavy engines (weighing over 70 tons each) of the Barry Company (by whom the traffic over the new line is to be worked) to run daily backwards and forwards over the viaduct, and on the occasions when I inspected the line four of these engines (two on each track) passed several times over it and no movement or settlement of either the arches, piers, or foundations could be detected.

I am informed that borings have been taken alongside of each pier, and these appear to shew that the foundations of all the piers have been carried down to solid limestone rock.

Drawings of the sections of the bore holes shewing the strata through which the foundations have been carried, have been furnished by the Company, and the engineers have given me their assurance that these borings were in all cases carried down to a depth of 30 ft below the foundations and that nothing but solid rock was met with at that depth. Tests have also been made by Messrs Kirkaldy of the resistance to crushing of limestone rock taken from a cutting adjacent to the viaduct which indicate that rock of this description is very hard.

The stability of the viaduct depends on the foundations and the structure will require carefully watching for some months to come. It is probable that if any further settlement takes place it will be of a gradual nature, and a watchman should be appointed, whose sole duty will be to patrol the viaduct (above and below) between the passage of trains, so that the slightest movement, should such occur, will be immediately detected. At the same time the speed over the viaduct should be limited to 20 miles an hour, and if these precautions are adopted, the use of the viaduct for traffic may, I consider, be permitted. At the end of 3 months it will be desirable for a further inspection of the structure to be made.

There are two tunnels on the railway the lengths of which are 537 and 68 yds respectively. They are lined throughout with masonry and the work seems to me in places to be very coarse. There are six culverts of diameters varying from 6 ft to 3 ft, one of these, viz that at 0 miles 78 chains, has settled down in the centre owing to the weight of the embankment above it. It is said that this settlement occured two years ago, and that nothing further has happened since then. But this culvert should be frequently examined, until all probability of further settlement is passed.

The other works appear to be standing satisfactorily and to possess sufficient stability, though in the case of some of the larger bridges the brick arches appear somewhat light, especially as they are in all cases but one, laid in lime mortar and not in cement and in some instances have very heavy embankments above them.

There are five stations on the line, beside the terminal stations at Barry and Bridgend, viz, Rhoose, Aberthaw, Gileston, Llantwit Major and Southerndown Road.

They all have two platforms each of which is 400 ft long, 3 ft high, and with an overhang of 12 ins. The accommodation at each station is excellent and includes conveniences for both sexes.

The signalling arrangements of the new line apart from those of the junctions with the Barry Railway and GWR, which have been separately reported on are carried out in the following signal boxes, viz:

1.	Barry Sidings Box	37 levers in use	15 levers spare
2.	Rhoose Station	19 levers in use	5 levers spare
3.	Aberthaw	31 levers in use	6 levers spare
4.	Gileston	17 levers in use	4 levers spare
5.	Llantwit Major	31 levers in use	6 levers spare
6.	Southerndown	31 levers in use	6 levers spare
7.	Bridgend curve	62 levers in use	12 levers spare

I noted a few desirable alterations and additions in the interlocking which I am informed are being carried out, and which it is not necessary to describe in detail now, as a re-inspection of the line will be necessary hereafter, when I shall be able to ascertain whether the requirements have been attended to.

I feel some hesitation in recommending the Board of Trade to give their final authority for the opening of the line for passenger traffic until sufficient time has elapsed to enable the stability of the works to be satisfactorily established. I suggested to the Engineers of the Company that it would be advisable to open the line for goods traffic only for a few months but this course did not commend itself to them.

I have, therefore, given the matter very careful consideration and would recommend the Board of Trade to authorise the opening of the line for passenger traffic for a period of three months, subject to the following conditions:

(a) the maximum speed on any part of the line not to exceed 25 miles an hour.

(b) the speed over the viaduct not to exceed 20 miles an hour.

(c) the speed over the river Daw bank, and the clay bank at Bridgend not to exceed 15 miles an hour. These embankments to be examined twice daily.

(d) the employment of a competent watchman on the viaduct whose sole duty shall be to examine the structure above and below (arches, piers, abutments etc.) between the passage of trains, so that any settlement or movement shall be immediately detected.

(e) the completion of the minor details such as coupling up of signal wires and point rods the provision of hand railing at the bridges, screens to urinals etc. etc.

(f) a re-inspection of the line at the end of three months from this date.

(g) the submission of plans of the signalling arrangements.

The conditional sanction of the Board of Trade, as recommended by Lt Colonel Yorke, was forwarded to the VoGR on 11th November, 1897.

Notwithstanding Lt Colonel Yorke's reservations, planning went ahead for the introduction of the passenger train service, which was arranged for 1st December, 1897. At least two special passenger trains worked over the VoGR prior to this date: on 18th September, 1897 the Directors of the company travelled over the line; and on 24th September a special train conveyed members of the Bristol Channel Centre of the Institute of Marine Engineers from Barry to Bridgend. On 25th November, 1897 detailed instructions for working the new railway were sent out by the ByR General Manager, Richard Evans. All was set for the formal opening of the VoGR.

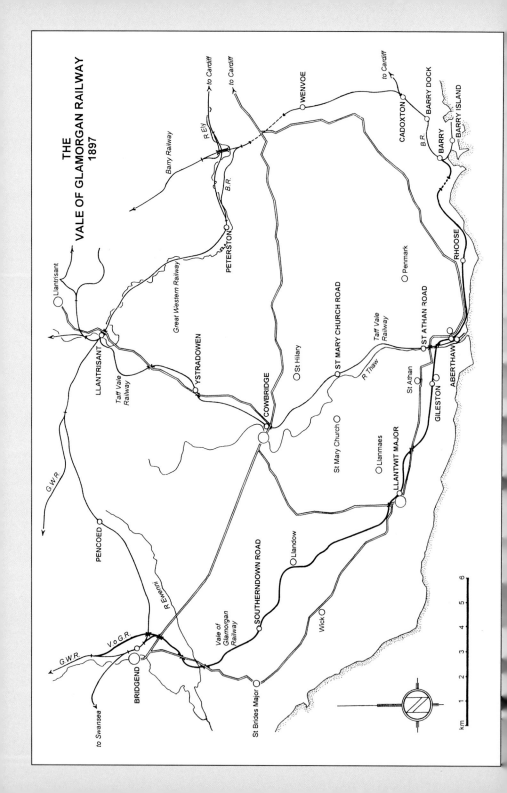

Chapter Four

Celebration and Despair

Wednesday 1st December, 1897 was, according to the *Western Mail*, an occasion for 'considerable public rejoicings' along the route of the VoGR. The first pasenger trains left Barry for Bridgend at 7.0 am, driven by E. Parry, with J. Hayward as guard. On board was an impressive set of dignitaries including, from the ByR Co., Richard Evans, General Manager, H.J. Vincent, Deputy Chairman, James Bell, Engineer, J.H. Hosgood, locomotive superintendent, and C. Butler, railway inspector, together with W. Thomas J.P., Chairman of Barry Urban District Council. The train was hauled by a ByR class 'G' 0-4-4T No. 68, which was profusely decorated with the shields of the Houses of Windsor, Talbot, Aberdare and Dunraven, and the Royal and Prince of Wales standards. At Llantwit Major the town had, we are told by the *Western Mail*, 'assumed quite a holiday appearance'. Crowds thronged the station and church bells rang out in honour of the new arrival. In the afternoon, through the generosity of Mr Vachell, the Cardiff solicitor, the children of the town were entertained to tea, whilst in the evening their elders were guests at a public dinner.

Station masters were appointed from other stations on the Barry system. The new appointees were: at Rhoose, G. Ashton, late of Barry; at Aberthaw, T. Howells, late of St Fagans; at Gileston, T. Cule (who was later to became the second station master at Llantwit Major), late of Dinas Powis; at Llantwit Major, W. B. Fletcher, late of Cadoxton; and at Southerndown Road, W. T. Nicholls, late of Barry.

The initial signs were quite encouraging. In the first month, despite the rather limited train service and temporary speed restriction of 25 mph over the line, nearly 15,000 passengers were carried. As there was no Sunday service this represented about 570 passengers per day, or 70 for each of the eight trains which made up the daily service between Barry and Bridgend. During the same period 5,700 wagon loads of coal (equivalent to about 200 train loads) had been conveyed over the line to Barry Docks.

There had been one piece of bad news, however. On 16th December, 1897 the embankment at the Barry end of Porthkerry viaduct had settled and begun to slip, with the first pier and the second arch showed signs of being affected. Remedial measures, involving the placing of large stones at the 'toe' of the slope and between piers Nos. 13 and 14 (the first and second from the Barry end), were quickly adopted.

This action appeared to have contained this particular difficulty, but on the morning of Monday 10th January, 1898 came news of a far more serious problem. The watchman employed at the viaduct, having come on duty at 6.00 am, detected a more serious slip in the embankment, together with a crack in the parapet wall and signs of settlement over the third pier from the Barry end. The exact timing of this discovery is not altogether clear. The Board of Trade report into the failure of the viaduct implies that it was discovered when the watchman came on duty, i.e. at 6.00 am. However, this would have been some time before the arrival of the first down passenger train, the 7.00 am departure from Barry, which crossed the viaduct at the normal time. Either this train was allowed to pass, even though the failure had been detected, or the discovery occurred after its passage, which is thought more likely. In any event, the ByR Engineer, James Bell, was quickly summoned and made his way to the stricken structure, accompanied by the company's locomotive engineer, Mr Waddell, on board 'C' class 2-4-0T No. 52. It appears that No. 52 was taken, somewhat gingerly, over the viaduct, but that caution advised against its return by the same route. It was necessary, therefore, for No.52 to make its way back to Barry, via Bridgend and Peterston Junction. The first up passenger train was stopped on the western side of the viaduct, from where its passengers were obliged to cross on foot to join a special train, which had been brought up to the eastern end, for their journey on to Barry. This arrangement continued for the rest of Monday, the *Western Mail* noting that the place had acquired the colloquial title of 'Porthkerry Viaduct Foot Junction'. The following morning, however, it was considered advisable to discontinue this practice in favour of a service of horse brakes between Barry and Rhoose stations, provided by Woodhams of Barry. Coal traffic was diverted via the South Wales main line and Peterston Junction.

On 12th January, 1898 several VoGR Directors visited the viaduct and examined the defective portion. No doubt this visit provided useful background for the consideration of the problem at the VoGR Board meeting on 14th January, 1898, when it was agreed that John Wolfe Barry, in his capacity as the company's Consulting Engineer, and John Strain, the arbitrator, should be requested to inspect the viaduct and report their views on the matter.

It was evident that restoration of the viaduct would take some time, but it was also recognised that there was an immediate need to restore the continuity of the railway between Barry and Bridgend in order to generate much needed income. On 18th January, 1898 the VoGR Engineers completed a report dealing with alternative ways of providing a temporary link in place of the viaduct. A timber structure could be built alongside part or all of the viaduct, which could then be repaired without interfering with the traffic of the railway. This would cost £4,000 for a half-length structure, or double that for the whole of the viaduct. Alternatively, a temporary diversion, avoiding the viaduct altogether, could be provided at a cost of about £2,500, exclusive of land acquisition; the Engineers recommended this as the better solution. A somewhat different approach was advocated by Mr Strain, the arbitrator, who advised that the arch between Nos. 13 and 14 piers should be supported on centering and scaffolding, that several others should be stayed with timbers, and that concrete ribs should be inserted under the two damaged arches. Fortunately for the aesthetic qualities of the viaduct Strain's solution did not find favour, although the only immediate action, authorised by the VoGR Board at its meeting on 19th January, 1898, was the digging of bore holes adjacent to the failed piers.

It was, of course, necessary to inform the Board of Trade of the failure of the viaduct. Lt Colonel Yorke returned to the scene on 20th January, 1898 to inspect the structure. His first concern was that it might collapse; he noted that 'it was at once apparent that the condition of the work was critical'. The upper part of the viaduct, near the affected pier, had bulged out and one of the arches appeared ready to fall at any moment. As a result of these concerns action was taken to lighten the weight on the defective arches by removing some of the superstructure. This appeared to produce the desired effect as no further movement took place.

Lt Colonel Yorke completed his report on 6th April, 1898. In it he was able to quote at length from the record of his earlier inspection, referring, in particular, to his misgivings concerning the stability of the viaduct and to the precautions he had recommended. He noted that, at his earlier inspection, he had been assured that there was at least 30 ft of solid rock beneath each pier. However, bore holes which had since made by Tilley & Sons, artesian well sinkers, had revealed a very serious discrepancy at No. 13 Pier (which had sunk by 17 inches earlier in the month). Whereas the original section showed this pier to have foundations 10 ft deep resting on solid rock, extending to a depth of at least 51 ft 8 in. below the surface, Tilleys' section revealed an altogether different picture. This showed the pier to be resting on clay and shale to a depth of 27 ft, followed by 4 in. of rock and 4 ft 8 in. of broken shale. Mixed beds of rock and shale were not reached until 32 ft below the surface. In addition, the foundations were a good deal shallower than those of the adjacent piers, which, as Yorke pointed out, had failed during construction, with one pier having been rebuilt with deeper foundations, and two others having been underpinned. Yorke concluded that pier No. 13 had failed because it was resting on clay and shale rather than rock. He did not consider that the slippage of the embankment had contributed to this failure, which, in his view, would have occurred in any event, given the nature of the ground. He also found a number of discrepancies in the sections relating to four other piers, but none of these showed any signs of settlement. Finally, and most tellingly, he asserted that had he been supplied with the Tilleys' bore hole results in the previous October, he would not have passed the railway for passenger traffic.

To return to the immediate problems faced by the VoGR Directors: on 3rd February, 1898 the Board approved a plan of a temporary loop line at Porthkerry, avoiding the viaduct. The contract for the works was awarded to Price & Wills (contractors for Barry New Dock), for £5,647. Construction started on 15th February, 1898, and was extremely rapid, no doubt spurred on by the need to replace lost revenue. On 1st April, 1898 Sir James Szlumper reported that the loop line was within a day or two of completion, and that a Board of Trade inspection had been arranged for the following week.

Lt Colonel Yorke completed his report of this inspection on 19th April, 1898. The new loop line was single track, 2 m. 44 ch. in length, and followed the contours of the land, more or less on the surface, but with cuttings at each end. The ruling gradient was 1 in 40 and the sharpest curve had a radius of six chains. All curves of less than 10 chains radius were fitted with check rails. There was one underbridge, of timber construction, with seven spans of 11 ft 6 in. each. Two public roads were crossed on the level. Entry to the loop line was controlled by signal boxes at its extremities: Porthkerry East, with nine levers, all in use; and Porthkerry West, with 15 levers, again all in use. The line itself was worked on the Electric Train Staff system. Lt Colonel Yorke concluded his report by noting that, considering its temporary nature, the loop line was 'substantially constructed'. Nevertheless, he recommended that a 10 mph speed restriction be imposed, and that the heaviest locomotives be excluded from working the line. Board of Trade approval for the use of the loop line for passenger traffic was passed to the VoGR Co. on 22nd April, 1898,

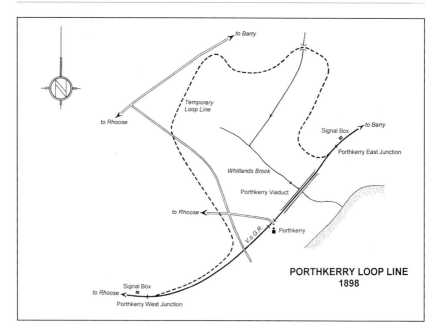

PORTHKERRY LOOP LINE
1898

enabling the line to be brought into use for such traffic on 25th April, 1898.

It will be recalled that one of Lt. Colonel Yorke's conditions, as set out in his report of 10th November, 1897, was that there should be a re-inspection of the VoGR after three months. His re-inspection report was completed on 27th April, 1898, but was somewhat overshadowed by events at Porthkerry. In it he recommended that the temporary speed restriction be lifted, and that full sanction be given for the use of the line by passenger traffic, with the obvious exception of Porthkerry viaduct.

With traffic able to make use of the Porthkerry loop line, consideration was then given to the best means of restoring a permanent route. On 26th April, 1898 James Bell reported on the two options available to the company: either to build a permanent diversion for the railway, or to repair the viaduct. Bell strongly urged that the viaduct should be repaired. This recommendation, together with the views of Sir James Szlumper and Mr Strain, was considered by the VoGR Board on 12th May, 1898. Having examined the various alternatives, the Directors decided that the viaduct should be repaired, and instructed James Bell to proceed with the work with 'all possible despatch'.

Bell set about his task with a will, but soon discovered that the condition of the viaduct was rather worse than he had expected. Very poor quality concrete had been used for the foundations of the piers, and this, in a number of cases, was giving rise to further subsidence and movement in certain arches. In addition, the parapet walls were cracking, evidence of movement across the whole of the structure. The situation appeared to be so bad that Bell felt obliged to comment, in a report prepared on 8th September, 1898, but not presented to his Directors, that, 'If I had had any idea that the old work was so bad I would never have advised the patching up of the viaduct, but instead would have advised it being entirely taken down and rebuilt.'

Nevertheless, work proceeded apace, under Bell's supervision, to restore the viaduct to a fit state for traffic. Restoration claimed the life of one of the workmen, who, on 25th July, 1898, fell from the structure, fracturing his skull. He was rushed to the nearby cottage hospital, but died shortly afterwards.

Finance for the reconstruction of the viaduct was provided by the ByR Co. on the basis of its friendly relations with the VoGR Co. However, this was only an interim measure as powers were sought for additional capital in the VoGR Bill in the 1899 Session of Parliament. The Act, which received Royal Assent on 6th June, 1899, included authority to raise additional capital to the sum of £120,000, with £40,000 in increased borrowing powers. It also contained retrospective powers for the construction of the Porthkerry loop line.

With only the fixing of some coping stones remaining to be completed, the viaduct was reopened to mineral traffic on 8th January, 1900. On 13th March 1900, at the request of the VoGR Co., Lt Colonel Yorke made an inspection of the restored structure. In his report, dated 4th April, 1900, he was full of praise for the quality of the work, in marked contrast to his views on the viaduct, as originally built, commenting that 'The restoration of the viaduct has been carried out with much skill and completeness by Mr James Bell, Engineer of the Barry Railway'. Lt Colonel Yorke found that substantial improvements had been made: the foundations of two abutments and five piers had been underpinned and deepened; the pier that had failed on 6th January, 1898 had been entirely rebuilt; the bearing areas of the foundations of all of the piers had been doubled, so as to halve the load on them; and nine arches had been entirely rebuilt, and the remaining seven strengthened. Finally, the viaduct had been lengthened at each end, with two extra arches at the Bridgend end and one at the Barry end.

Lt Colonel Yorke had made several visits to the site during the period of reconstruction, and could, therefore, testify to the 'very thorough manner' in which the work had been carried out. He could find no signs of settlement or movement, and concluded his report by stating that the 'design of the viaduct is vastly improved and strengthened', and that 'no fears need . . . now be felt as to its stability'. He had no hesitation, therefore, in recommending that the Board of Trade approve of the viaduct, as rebuilt. This approval was forwarded to the VoGR Co. on 9th April, 1900.

Passenger trains started using the viaduct again on 9th April, 1900. With its usefulness at an end Porthkerry loop line was soon taken up and the land restored to its former use. Nevertheless, reminders of this short-lived, but very necessary, railway can still be found, with a short length of cutting surviving at the Barry end of the viaduct and a gradually rising shelf cut into the side of the cutting to the east of Rhoose.

An inevitable consequence of the collapse of Porthkerry viaduct was a protracted arbitration dispute between the VoGR Co. and the contractors, Pethick Bros, which was adjudicated by Sir James Szlumper. Sir James made his award on 7th March, 1901: whereas the contractors had claimed a total of £148,700 against the VoGR Co., they were to receive only £29,716. They were also obliged to pay the railway company the costs of the counter- claim.

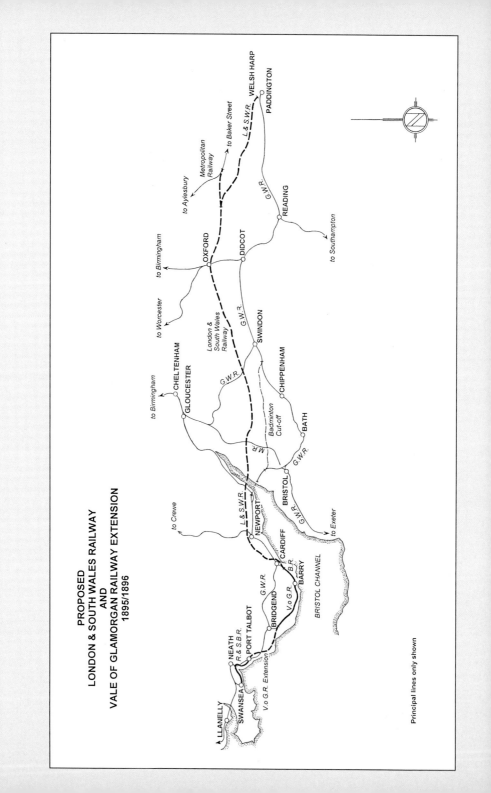

PROPOSED
LONDON & SOUTH WALES RAILWAY
AND
VALE OF GLAMORGAN RAILWAY EXTENSION
1895/1896

Principal lines only shown

Chapter Five

Unfulfilled Ambitions

As has been seen, the principal objective behind the promotion of the VoGR was to provide a link between the coalfield of the Bridgend valleys and Barry Dock. However, the company also developed ambitions in two other directions: firstly, for an extension of the railway to the west of Bridgend; and secondly, for a connection from the company's 'main line' to the village of Southerndown on the coast, about two miles west of Southerndown Road station. These two ambitions, at opposite ends of the spectrum in terms of the scale of the schemes involved, were to become recurring themes during the pre-Grouping years, but both were destined to remain unfulfilled.

Westward Extension

A westward extension of their railway appears to have been a very early ambition of the VoGR promoters. At a meeting on 25th October, 1889 they gave consideration to the question of an extension to Porthcawl, but agreed to defer a decision, following advice from Thomas Forster Brown, who anticipated difficultes in respect of certain GWR sidings at the intended terminus. Just what this extension was meant to achieve, however, remains a mystery.

In 1895 the VoGR, then still under construction, became involved in a grandiose proposal for a new trunk route between London and South Wales, competitive with that of the GWR. The success of the London Extension Bill of the Manchester Sheffield and Lincolnshire Railway (later Great Central Railway) in 1892 had provided an incentive for similar schemes elsewhere, but there had long been dissatisfaction in certain quarters with the GWR's monopoly of traffic between London and South Wales. Over the years various proposals had been put forward to challenge the GWR's position, but none had progressed very far. In November 1895 plans were deposited for the 'London and South Wales Railway', to run from a junction with the ByR, at Cogan, to London. The proposed railway was to pass to the south of the GWR in Cardiff, then via a route to the north of Newport, to cross the Severn at Aust by means of a bridge 3,300 yds long. From there it was to run via Thornbury, Malmesbury, Cricklade and Oxford to Welsh Harp, near Hendon, with a branch to Great Missenden to join the Metropolitan Railway. Running powers were sought over the ByR, VoGR, Port Talbot Railway, Rhondda and Swansea Bay Railway and the railways of the Swansea Harbour Trust (SHT). Prominent amongst the promoters of the London & South Wales Railway scheme were various luminaries in the ByR Co., with the Barry connection also being apparent in the engineering staff, with Sir James Szlumper, Thomas Forster Brown and William Szlumper listed as the Engineers, and John Wolfe Barry as Consulting Engineer.

It should be remembered that at the time of this proposal traffic between South Wales and London was still being worked via Bath. The opening of the

Severn Tunnel in 1886 had obviated the long detour via Gloucester, but there was still discontent over the lack of a truly direct route between South Wales and the Metropolis.

Clearly acting in concert with this proposal, the VoGR Board, at its meeting on 1st November, 1895, resolved to deposit a Bill for the westward extension of its railway. This envisaged a line from the VoGR at Ewenny, passing close to Porthcawl, to junctions with the PTR and R&SBR near Port Talbot, with running powers being sought over the PTR, R&SBR and SHT lines. This move had been foreshadowed on 28th October, 1895, when Edward Davies and Sir James Szlumper had inspected the Swansea passenger and goods stations of the R&SBR, together with the site proposed for that company's new station in the town.

Plans were also deposited by the PTR for links with the R&SBR and to intercept the VoGR extension, in addition to its main proposal, an independent connection between Port Talbot and the Ogmore Valleys. The London & South Wales scheme was also considered by the R&SBR Board on 12th November, 1895, when it was agreed that the company might become involved in the creation of a new trunk route, but that it should not take part in a purely local arrangement.

The GWR quickly responded to the threat of a competitive route for its lucrative South Wales traffic by bringing forward proposals for a direct line between Wootton Bassett and Patchway, the so-called 'Badminton Cut-off'. This counter-move cut the legs from under the London & South Wales scheme, and an accommodation was soon reached between its promoters and the GWR. Under agreements, dated 10th January, 1896, with the ByR and with the London & South Wales promoters, the GWR addressed a wide range of contentious issues relating to South Wales, in exchange for the abandonment of the London & South Wales scheme. The latter, and the VoGR Bills were then withdrawn. The GWR obtained its Act for the Badminton Cut-off on 7th August, 1896, and the new line was opened for goods throughout on 1st May, 1903, and to passengers on 1st July of that year.

The London & South Wales was described, at the time, as a 'wild-cat scheme', and was undoubtedly a 'paper' proposal, designed to wring concessions from the GWR, in which it was most successful. However, railway history is full of 'paper' schemes which, through miscalculation or unforeseen events, became 'real' railways. If different circumstances had prevailed, the VoGR could well have become part of a through route from London to Swansea, in direct competition with that of the GWR. The VoGR would have provided easier gradients for freight traffic, but its curvature would have precluded anything approaching high speed. A westward extension of the VoGR would also have enabled the ByR to tap the emerging anthracite coalfield to the north-west of Neath, but it was to be another 10 years before the Barry Co. was to reach out again in this direction.

The coalfield in question was not well served by existing railways. On 6th July, 1895 an Act had been obtained for the Neath Pontardawe and Brynamman Railway (NP&BR), connecting the Swansea and Neath line of the GWR, near Neath, with Brynamman, and opening up the coalfield. Running powers over the authorised railways were granted to the GWR and the Midland Railway, and on 14th August, 1896 a further Act empowered the NP&BR to enter into working and traffic agreements with the GWR. A third Act, on 25th July, 1898, authorised the construction of two branch lines at Pontardawe, and granted an

extension of time for the lines authorised by the 1895 Act. However, the
NP&BR promoters were unable to raise the necessary funds, despite the
amicable relations existing with the GWR. Approaches were also made to the
R&SBR. On 27th May, 1896 the R&SBR Board indicated that the it would be
willing to work the NP&BR for a percentage of gross receipts, but was not
prepared to guarantee interest on capital expended. A proposal that the R&SBR
acquire the undertaking of the NP&BR was rejected on 1st December, 1899.

Relations between the NP&BR promoters and the GWR deteriorated
markedly in 1902 and 1903 when the GWR put forward a rival scheme for
railways between the Swansea and Neath line and Gwaun-Cae-Gurwen, near
Brynamman. The NP&BR promoters sought the renewal of the powers of their
1895 Act, together with authority to raise additional capital and for further
borrowing powers. Although the Neath Co. prevailed in this contest, its Act
receiving Royal Assent on 11th August, 1903, the promoters were still unable to
command the necessary support, and so no further progress was made.

In 1897 Archibald Hood, then Vice-Chairman of the ByR Co., together with
fellow Director T.R. Thompson, had inspected the route of the proposed
NP&BR and had concluded that it offered good prospects as a feeder for Barry
Docks. Although nothing came of this particular visit, as far as the Barry Co.
was concerned, Thompson and another Barry Director, Robert Forrest,
subsequently became Directors of the NP&BR Co. Hood, Thompson and
Forrest were also Directors of the VoGR Co.

As will by now be quite clear, the Barry Co. was always on the look-out for
fresh opportunities or threats to such opportunities, and in 1906 a noticeable
warming in the relationship between the GWR and the R&SBR set alarm bells
ringing at its headquarters in Barry. In 1903 these two companies had made an
agreement whereby GWR trains between Briton Ferry and Swansea could make
use of the R&SBR's Neath River Bridge, thereby avoiding the lengthy detour,
via Neath, and reversal, previously required to reach the Swansea and Neath
line. This arrangement was soon seen to be of mutual benefit and led directly
to an agreement, dated 1st July, 1906 (but effective from 1st January of that
year), whereby the GWR, for most practical purposes, took over the working
and management of the R&SBR.

To the ByR Co. this agreement appeared to presage full amalgamation of the
two companies, a move which would have severely restricted any prospect of
access to the Neath coalfield. On 20th July, 1906 the Barry Directors agreed to
confer with their counterparts on the Port Talbot Railway Board regarding the
threatened 'amalgamation' of the R&SBR with the GWR, which they saw as
hostile to the PTR Co.'s, as well as their own, interests. At the same meeting the
future of the proposed NP&BR was considered, and it was agreed that it was
desirable for the Barry Co. to take steps to keep this scheme alive.

Discussions then took place with representatives of the PTR regarding the
possibilities of amalgamation with or the lease of its undertaking by the ByR
Co., or the entering into of a working and traffic agreement similar to that
already in place with the VoGR Co., but these proved fruitless. The Barry
General Manager, Edward Lake, was of the view that, in the case of
amalgamation of the two companies, it would be essential to build a connecting

railway between the VoGR and the PTR, either from Coity Junction to Cefn Junction, near Kenfig Hill, or from Ewenny to Margam, and also desirable to obtain running powers over the R&SBR.

With powers for the construction of their authorised railways due to lapse, it was essential that the NP&BR promoters obtain an Act for an extension of time in the 1907 Session. Barry support would greatly assist the passage of such a Bill, and on 5th April, 1907, faced with signs of an increasingly cordial relationship between the GWR and the PTR, the Barry Board instructed Edward Lake to state, in evidence in favour of the NP&BR Bill, that the ByR Co. was prepared to assist in raising the necesary capital. A yet stronger commitment to the scheme emerged on 29th May, 1907, when it was agreed to authorise an agreement with the NP&BR along the lines of that with the VoGR. With Mr Lake's evidence providing the necessary endorsement, the NP&BR obtained its extension of time, the Act receiving Royal Assent on 21st August, 1907.

This Act kept the NP&BR alive, but the ByR Co. needed a greater degree of control over the scheme. On 1st November, 1907 its Directors agreed to include in a Parliamentary notice powers of the 'widest possible character', in relation to the NP&BR, including provisions for taking over the undertaking, working the railway and guaranteeing payment of interest on capital expended. However, events elsewhere were conspiring against Barry ambitions. On 24th January, 1908 an agreement was entered into between the GWR and the PTR (effective from 1st January, 1908) similar to that already existing between the GWR and the R&SBR. Thus although its Act of 1st August, 1908 gave the Barry Co. powers to subscribe towards the capital of, and enter into working and traffic agreements with the NP&BR, nothing came of this particular enactment. The company was effectively boxed in by the agreements concluded between the GWR and the R&SBR and the PTR, and its hopes of reaching the Neath anthracite fields were never to be realised. Matters were finally sealed when, on 18th August, 1911, the GWR obtained an Act for railways between its Swansea District Railway (opened throughout on 14th July, 1913) at Felin Fran and Gwaun-Cae-Gurwen, although, with the outbreak of World War I, only part of this scheme was completed. Powers for the construction of the NP&BR lapsed in 1912.

The final proposal for a westward extension from the VoGR came not from the ByR, but from the GWR. With the end of hostilities in 1918 it seemed not unreasonable to expect traffic on the railways of South Wales to revert to its pre-war rates of growth. Following discussions between officers of the GWR and the Minister of Transport and his civil servants, a memorandum was drawn up, in March 1920, by the railway company, which advocated substantial new works in South Wales and other parts of the GWR system, to relieve congestion and cope with expected traffic growth. An important part of this programme was to be the construction of a new railway from the South Wales main line, near Peterston, to Margam, following a very similar route, west of Ewenny (where a connection was to be made with the VoGR), to that envisaged in the VoGR proposals of 1895/6. The course of this proposed new main line had been surveyed before the war, but a later survey was confined to a new route between the South Wales main line, to the east of Bridgend, and Margam. If a junction were to be provided between this line and the VoGR, at Ewenny, then use could be made of the VoGR to reach the new railway. However, the post-war world was not a friendly place for such expansionist dreams, and with the approach of the Grouping, and the prospect of alternative routes which the absorption of lesser local companies would bring with it, nothing more was heard of this bold proposal.

The Southerndown Connection

Southerndown, with its sheltered sandy bay and dramatic cliffs, had been a popular destination for tourists from the 1860s onwards. A service of horse brakes had linked the village with the GWR station in Bridgend during the summer months from at least 1890. Southerndown was clearly seen as having the potential to develop into an important resort, catering perhaps for a more discriminating clientele. To this end two large hotels - the Dunraven and the Marine - were built to accommodate the expected influx of visitors.

However, in the late 1890s budding resorts needed a rail link if they were to prosper and grow. It is also clear that in choosing the site for Southerndown Road station the VoGR Directors had in mind a connection between their railway and Southerndown. The passing of the Light Railway Act in 1896 provided the basis on which an economical rail link could achieved. On 17th September, 1897 the ByR Board agreed to give its consent should the VoGR decide to make a light railway from Southerndown Road station to Southerndown. Surveys were undertaken and notices prepared for an application to the Light Railway Commissioners for the 'Vale of Glamorgan Light Railway'. The line was to be about 2¾ miles long, with a ruling gradient of 1 in 50, and an estimated cost of £13,500. It was to cross three roads on the level, but if bridges were insisted on instead of level crossings the cost of the line would be increased by £4,500.

The notice for the proposed light railway was presented to the VoGR Board on 4th November, 1897. However, prospects for the scheme rapidly became very clouded when one of the Directors, T.R. Thompson, reported on the unsafisfactory outcome of his interview with the principal landowner, Lord Dunraven. In response to this 'unexpected opposition', the company's Engineer, Sir James Szlumper, had prepared a report on an alternative route for the light railway. This was to leave the VoGR main line at Ewenny, and follow the valley of the River Ogmore to Ogmore-by-Sea, before proceeding along the coast to Southerndown. The total length of this line would be about 5 miles, with an estimated cost of £20,000. If, however, an additional curve, towards Barry, was provided at the junction at Ewenny, the cost of the proposed railway would be increased by £3,000. Having considered this alternative route and other factors, the Board decided to take no further action that year to promote the light railway.

The ambition to reach Southerndown still persisted, however. On 3rd September, 1898 the *Railway Times* reported that a great deal of property had been sold in the locality, with the result that it would be possible to build a light railway to Southerndown 'scarcely touching' the Dunraven estate. Nevertheless, no further progress was made with the idea of a rail link to Southerndown.

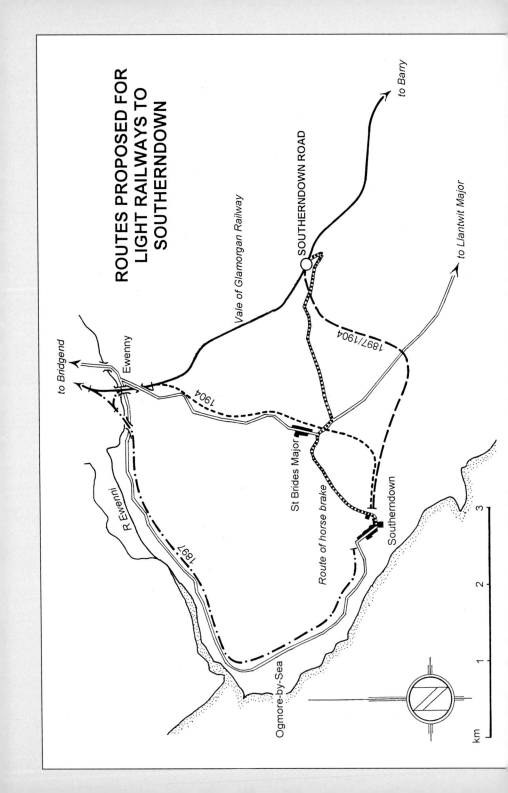

ROUTES PROPOSED FOR LIGHT RAILWAYS TO SOUTHERNDOWN

to Barry

SOUTHERNDOWN ROAD

Vale of Glamorgan Railway

to Llantwit Major

1897/1904

1904

to Bridgend

Ewenny

R Ewenni

St Brides Major

Route of horse brake

1897

Southerndown

Ogmore-by-Sea

km

N

However, it was still felt that there was a need for some sort of connection between the VoGR and Southerndown. The brake service from Bridgend was only of benefit to the GWR; a similar service from Southerndown Road, on the other hand, would encourage visitors from Cardiff and beyond to travel via Barry to Southerndown. On 2nd May, 1899 the ByR General Manager, Richard Evans, informed his Directors that he had met Mr Davies of the Marine Hotel, Southerndown, on the subject of a horse brake service between Southerndown Road station and Southerndown. Mr Davies had offered to operate such a service, meeting three trains each way, provided he received a guaranteed sum of £3 per week from the ByR Co. This proposition was accepted by the Barry Traffic Committee, and the service was introduced later that month. During the first season, which lasted about five months, 641 single and 549 return tickets were issued for the brake service, compared with a total of 14,385 passengers handled at Southerndown Road station in the eight months ending 31st September, 1899.

Mr Davies's horse brake service was seen, at the time, as a 'temporary arrangement', and in February 1904 the question of an improved link to Southerndown again came under consideration. Initially thoughts were directed towards the possibility of a motor bus service between Southerndown Road station and Southerndown. Information on the operating costs of such a service was obtained from the GWR, but these were found to be excessive, suggesting yearly running costs of £300 which would dwarf the expected annual income of only £60. On 31st March, 1904 Richard Evans reported that further enquiries had confirmed these figures. He also noted that during the preceding season the brake service had met nine trains on Mondays to Saturdays and six on Sundays. The company had lost £16 6s. 8d. over the whole season, with Mr Davies receiving a guaranteed sum of £3 5s. per week. Mr Evans went on to report that he had been in communication with Mr Chick of Westgate Street, Cardiff, who had offered to work the service with a 20-seat brake for £3 10s. per week. This offer was accepted by the Barry Board on 7th April, 1904, but at the same meeting Mr Evans was asked to look again at the question of a light railway to Southerndown.

Mr Evans estimated that the annual expenditure needed for a light railway would be £2,004 as against an income of £589. William Waddell, the ByR Engineer, had examined three possible routes for the line. One similar to that proposed in 1897 would cost £19,000, whilst a variation on this, following the opposite side of the valley up from Southerndown Road station, would cost £2,000 less. A third route, leaving the VoGR at Ewenny and following the dry valley southwards to St Brides Major, would cost £21,000, but would require the erection of platforms at the intended junction, and have a ruling gradient of 1 in 27, described by Mr Waddell as 'rather severe'. Having considered these alternatives on 2nd June, 1904, the Barry Directors instructed Mr Waddell to investigate the possibility of constructing a tramway between Bridgend and Southerndown. Mr Waddell found that this would cost £30,000, and would tend to encourage traffic via the GWR rather than via Barry. On 30th June, 1904 the Barry Directors decided to postpone consideration of the matter until the local authorities were prepared to allow level crossings on the route.

Hopes for an improved link to Southerndown lingered on, however, and on 20th March, 1906 the *South Wales Daily News*, in a review of the prospects for a light railway to Southerndown, reported that the GWR was thinking of introducing a motor bus service between Bridgend and Southerndown. Reporting this rumour to his Directors on 13th June, 1906, Edward Lake, the Barry General Manager, advised that the GWR should be informed that such a move would be regarded as 'hostile' by the company.

A last faint echo of the light railway scheme came in July 1910 when Mr Lake reported that a Mr Nichols of Nantymoel had offered to sell to the company two cottages and a field at St Brides Major, on the route originally intended for the Vale of Glamorgan Light Railway between Southerndown Road station and Southerndown. Needless to say, this offer was not accepted.

Thus the only 'connection' that was made between the VoGR and Southerndown was the horse brake service from Southerndown Road station. Passengers were deposited from 'Chick's Brake' at Beach Road in Southerndown, and returned from the rear of the Marine Hotel. Tickets for the combined train and brake service, via Southerndown Road, were also available from Bridgend station. However, in January 1915 Thomas Rowe, who had previously operated a horse brake between Bridgend and Southerndown, introduced a motor bus on the direct route. On 31st March, 1922 Penybont District Council gave permission for the South Wales Commercial Motors Co. to run what was described as a 'cheap, efficient and comfortable' bus service between Bridgend, Ogmore-by-Sea and Southerndown. Although this ran for the summer season only, it followed the 'natural' route for traffic, one which was to see a great boom, with a variety of operators, in the inter-war years. It is unlikely that a light railway would have lasted very long in such an environment.

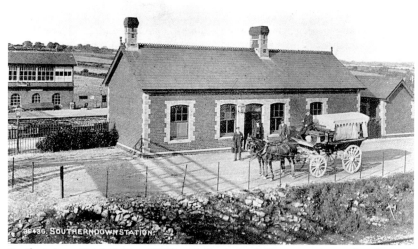

Southerndown Road station *c.* 1905, with the horse brake connection to the village of Southerndown.   *Author's Collection*

Chapter Six

Independent Days

Given the level of Barry Railway support and the presence of so many of that company's Directors on the VoGR Board, it must have seemed, at the opening of the line in 1897, that it would be only a matter of time before complete amalgamation occurred. Such a move appeared to be imminent when, on 1st July, 1898, the VoGR Board was informed of the Barry Co.'s terms for such a merger. The VoGR shareholders and debenture holders were to be offered equivalent Barry stock in exchange for their existing holdings, with the ByR Co. taking over unissued VoGR capital, together with its various obligations. On 5th August, 1898, the VoGR Board resolved to accept these terms, subject to the approval of the shareholders.

However, doubts then appear to have set in. The failure of Porthkerry viaduct had sapped confidence in the undertaking. In addition to the costs of repairing the viaduct and constructing the Porthkerry loop line, higher operating costs had resulted from the use of the loop line. Revenue had, of course, been lost, and there was uncertainty as to future prospects. Following a conference of the Boards of the two companies, held in Cardiff on 2nd November, 1898, at which a statement of the VoGR's assets and liabilities was considered, the Barry Directors decided that it would not be prudent, at that time, to proceed with any proposal for amalgamation.

By November 1902 prospects for amalgamation appeared good enough to justify the inclusion of enabling powers in the ByR Bill for the 1903 Session of Parliament. However, these provisions, which included authority for the sale or transfer of the VoGR to the ByR Co., were withdrawn following the breakdown of negotiations between the two companies. The VoGR Board had asked for better terms than the Barry Co. was prepared to grant. As an aside, it is difficult, to modern eyes at least, to see how, given the mutuality of the two Boards, problems with inside information and conflicts of interest could have been avoided in these negotiations.

After reaching this impasse no further attempt was made to merge the two companies, and the VoGR remained, legally at least, an independent concern through to the Grouping in 1922. In practical terms, however, it was always managed and worked as if it were an integral part of the ByR, and it certainly appeared as such.

The VoGR was built to carry coal, and its financial performance was largely dependent upon success on this front. This traffic had got off to a promising start with nearly 48,000 tons carried in the first month after the opening in 1897. However, the failure of Porthkerry viaduct had resulted in only 191,573 tons of coal being conveyed over the line in 1898. With the restoration of the viaduct, coal traffic grew rapidly to a total of 734,081 tons for the year 1899. The annual totals then stabilised and averaged about 700,000 tons per annum through to 1912, with a minimum of 574,428 tons recorded in 1905 and a maximum of 840,787 tons in 1902. Substantial tonnages also continued to be worked to Barry Docks, via

A busy scene at Barry station in pre-Grouping days, with a Vale of Glamorgan train about to depart in the centre of the picture. *L&GRP*

Class 'J' 2-4-2T No. 98 arrives at Barry on a Barry Island-Cardiff train in pre-Grouping days. *Lens of Sutton*

Peterston Junction, although this also included traffic brought on to the South Wales main line at Llantrisant, which could not have gone via the VoGR. However, the main competitor for Bridgend valleys traffic was the new Port Talbot Dock, which had opened in 1898. This dock, with its network of feeder railways, was very well placed for such traffic, and its coal exports quickly overtook the total handled by the VoGR. By 1905 the Port Talbot Railway was carrying twice as much coal as the VoGR, a ratio which increased to three to one by 1910, with traffic exceeding the combined totals for the VoGR and the Peterston Junction route for the first time in 1909. Clearly not all of this coal would have passed over the VoGR had the PTR not opened, but had it not the traffic of the VoGR undoubtedly would have been much greater.

The coal traffic carried over the VoGR formed a relatively small proportion of the export trade of Barry Docks, averaging about 10 per cent of its total in the period up to World War I. Reflecting the general increase in traffic in the years immediately before the war, the annual tonnage of coal over the VoGR grew to a peak of 1,136,533 tons in 1913, before falling back slightly in 1914, the peak year for coal exports from Barry Docks, when a total of over 11 million tons was shipped.

The vast bulk of VoGR coal traffic was transferred from the Llynfi and Ogmore section of the GWR at Coity Junction. Before 1904 traffic exchanged at Cowbridge Road Junction was almost insignificant, averaging under 4,000 tons per annum. This increased to 11,591 tons in 1905, and continued to rise to reach a peak of 104,031 tons in 1913, before falling back to 69,624 tons in 1914.

The limestone of the Vale of Glamorgan had long been used locally for the manufacture of lime and cement, but it was not until December 1888 that the first works of any size was opened. Connected to the Cowbridge and Aberthaw Railway on its opening in 1892, the Aberthaw Lime Works was reported to be disused at the opening of the VoGR in 1897, but was later reopened. However, apart from this and other similar works at St Mary Church Road and St Athan Road stations, the C&AR failed to develop the lime industry of the lower Thaw Valley, to the extent that its promoters had hoped. The VoGR, on the other hand, turned out to be much more successful in this respect. Early developments took place at opposite ends of the line, at Ewenny Quarry and Porthkerry Lime Works. Lime works were later opened at and near Southerndown Road station, and near Cowbridge Road Junction. A siding to the first large-scale modern cement works was opened at Rhoose in 1911, followed by one at Aberthaw Cement Works in 1913.

Local freight traffic was mainly agricultural in character, with domestic coal and shop goods also playing an important part, particularly at Llantwit Major. The railway company appears to have under-estimated the likely volume of goods traffic at this station, as in March 1899 the provision of two additional sidings was agreed. The opening of the station also encouraged the growth of cattle sales in the town, with the facilities for this traffic soon becoming inadequate. As a result there was a progressive increase in the number of pens provided at the station in the years up to World War I.

One problem faced in dealing with livestock traffic at Llantwit Major and other stations on the VoGR was the ByR's almost complete lack of cattle trucks.

Porthkerry viaduct in Barry Railway days with a five-coach train bound for Bridgend.
Author's Collection

Porthkerry viaduct with a Barry Railway passenger train made up of the ex-steam railcar 'Vestibule Set' and a pair of six-wheel coaches. *Author's Collection*

The curve immediately to the west of Porthkerry tunnel in Barry Railway days.
Author's Collection

BARRY RAILWAY.

NOTICE TO STAFF.

Installation of Shunting Gong, Porthkerry Tunnel.

At 9.0 a.m. on MONDAY NEXT, the 20th April, a Gong, which has been fixed about 200 yards inside the Porthkerry Tunnel, for the purpose of facilitating shunting operations at the West End of the Barry Sidings, will be brought into use.

The Gong will be connected with the Barry Sidings Signal Box, and will be operated by the Signalmen.

In connection with the Bell the following code will be used :—

Right Away	2 rings.
Stop	3 rings.
Move Ahead	4 rings.
Move back cautiously	5 rings.

Signalmen are required to make the beats in such a manner as will ensure the rings being clear and distinct from each other, and Enginemen are directed to pay particular attention to the code set out above.

Acknowledge receipt.

T. H. RENDELL,

GENERAL MANAGER.

BARRY DOCKS,
    April 17th, 1914.

Cir. No. 2882.   G.T. 323497.

(This instruction must be attached to Appendix No. 2, dated June, 1913).

Barry Railway Notice to Staff: Installation of shunting gong, Porthkerry tunnel.

Rhoose station in the early years of this century, looking towards Barry. The station building is in its original form with only two chimneys. *L&GRP*

Looking eastwards from Rhoose station, *c*. 1913, with the siding to the cement works on the right. Work on the Porthkerry-Rhoose down relief line (opened 1914) is underway just beyond the crossover in the centre of this view. *Lens of Sutton*

In November 1903 the General Manager, Richard Evans, brought this problem to the attention of his Directors, noting that the company owned only two vehicles, built by Brown & Marshall in 1896, which were totally inadequate for the traffic on offer. Trucks had been hired from the GWR and the TVR, but this had proved costly, and the arrangement with the latter company was also somewhat unreliable. Accordingly, a further six cattle trucks were ordered from Cravens Ltd in 1904. The resulting eight vehicles, together with a 'special cattle truck', also built by Cravens in 1904, were to make up the company's entire stock of cattle trucks at the Grouping in 1922.

The growth in traffic on the VoGR in the years leading up to the outbreak of World War I led to problems of congestion and delays on the line, particularly between Barry and Rhoose. In January 1914 it was decided that the most appropriate response was to provide a new down relief line between Porthkerry West and Rhoose station, a distance of nearly ¾ mile, at an estimated cost of £3,680. The new works were carried out at great speed, being brought into use on 30th August, 1914. However, it was not until 20th January, 1915 that the Board of Trade was informed that they were ready for inspection. This was carried out by Colonel E. Druitt, who completed his report on 8th February, 1915. The new relief line left the down line just before the lime works siding at Porthkerry, the junction itself being controlled by a new signal box, containing 21 levers, all in use. The lime works siding was realigned to join the new relief line. At Rhoose a trailing connection was made to the down line, just before the junction of the cement works siding. Colonel Druitt was satisfied with the arrangements and recommended that they be approved. As well as providing relief for the main line over this section, the new line enabled shunting to be carried out at the Porthkerry Lime Works and Rhoose Cement Works sidings with the minimum of interference with other traffic on the railway.

Four of the stations on the VoGR served the main settlements along its route, with the fifth, Southerndown Road, acting as a railhead for a number of nearby villages. However, certain other smaller communities, lying close to the railway, were not well-served. In particular, the long stretch of line between Llantwit Major and Southerndown Road stations soon attracted attention. This area was very thinly populated, with most of the villages being well to the south of the railway. However, there was one exception, the village of Llandow, situated about a third of the way between Llantwit Major and Southerndown Road. Although it was very close to the railway, Llandow suffered from very poor road access to the two nearest stations. Requests from the Llandow Parish Council for a halt were rejected in 1898 and 1901, but in 1905, in connection with the introduction of steam railcars on the VoGR, the provision of halts at Llandow and Fontigary, near Rhoose, was agreed. In the event these were not proceeded with, and in 1908 a further request from the parish council was turned down. A fourth application proved more successful, however, when, on 8th January, 1915, the ByR Co. approved the building of a halt, at an estimated cost of £250.

Llandow Halt was opened to passengers on Saturday 1st May, 1915, having been granted provisional sanction by the Board of Trade on 20th April, 1915.

Aberthaw station in Barry Railway days.

Lens of Sutton

Gileston station in Barry Railway days.

Lens of Sutton

BARRY RAILWAY.

NOTICE TO STAFF.

Application of Brakes at Gileston.

In connection with the above the following instructions will apply as from Monday next, the 21st instant.

When the Up Distant Signal at Gileston is at Danger, the Driver of a Goods or Mineral Train who requires brakes applied on wagons as well as on the Guard's van before descending the bank, will, upon approaching the brow of the bank, give two short blasts on the whistle to indicate to the Guard that he requires brakes applied. The Train will then be brought to a stand and the Guard will apply a few brakes on the wagons next to his van, as well as applying the brake on the van, in order to provide the additional brake power required by the Driver.

As soon as the Engine Driver has ascertained that the Signals at Gileston in advance of his train are at the "off" position he will stop the train, and the Guard must immediately raise the brakes applied on the wagons, return to his van, and give the Driver the signal to proceed. The Guard will release the brake of his van as soon as he considers it expedient to do so. In the event of the train being brought to a stand at the Home, Starting, or Advanced Starting Signal before the brakes have been raised, it will be the duty of the Guard to keep a sharp look out and raise the brakes as soon as the signal has been pulled "off."

Acknowledge receipt.

T. H. RENDELL.

Barry Docks,
    December 18th, 1914.

Cir. No. 3,064.   T. 343,988.

These instructions must be attached to page 67 of Appendix No. 2.

Barry Railway Notice to Staff: Application of brakes at Gileston.

The approach to Llantwit Major station *c.* 1900 with a cattle wagon in the end loading bay.
W. John Collection

An early view of Llantwit Major station from the Bridgend end of the platforms. *Lens of Sutton*

The inspection itself did not take place until the autumn, with Colonel Druitt's report being dated 15th October, 1915. Druitt found that two wooden platforms, each 130 ft long, had been provided, complete with wooden shelters. Additional signals, controlled from the existing signal box, had been installed, together with an electric bell for the protection of passengers crossing the line. This bell was operated by treadles placed on both lines 250 yds before the crossing. Being entirely satisfied with these arrangements, Colonel Druitt recommended the Board of Trade to approve of their use.

At the outbreak of World War I the nation's railways were brought under Government control through the medium of the Railway Executive Committee (REC), a body made up of representatives of the Board of Trade and the General Managers of the principal railway companies. The financial regime, which accompanied Government control, brought with it short-term problems for the VoGR, as on 23rd June, 1916 a request from the company for financial assistance to overcome a 'temporary difficulty' was rejected by the ByR Board.

Government control through the REC also brought with it a number of major changes to operating practices. In particular, the REC was anxious to improve the efficiency of freight operations. On 15th December, 1916 the ByR Traffic Committee heard that the Government had accepted a proposal for the common use of open wagons owned by the railway companies. Under this scheme the country was divided up between 12 major railway companies, with other lesser companies being allocated to each group as was deemed appropriate. The arrangements for the GWR group, which included the ByR, came into force on 2nd January, 1917. A similar proposal, involving the pooling of private owner wagons, met with very strong objections when it was reported at the ByR Traffic Committee on 2nd February, 1917, but was not proceeded with. In a move also designed to improve efficiency, the GWR suggested to the various local railway companies in South Wales that through working of coal traffic should be introduced, thereby avoiding the need to change engines at junctions. This suggestion was rejected outright by the Barry Traffic Committee on 16th February, 1917, the GWR being suspected of having ulterior motives which would have threatened the Barry Co.'s independence after the war.

In the case of passenger traffic, the REC was faced with two closely related problems. One was the growth of passenger traffic during the war years, and the other was the need to economise on the use of men and equipment in order that they might be diverted to the war effort. Fares were raised to discourage travel and services were reduced. On 1st January, 1917 the ByR, acting on instructions from the REC, increased its fares, excluding workmen's and season tickets, by no less than 60 per cent. This led to a dramatic fall in custom, but a small overall increase in revenue.

During the war years much of the export coal trade of Barry Docks was redirected to serve the needs of the Allied navies, but, nevertheless, traffic remained at a high level. The volume handled, coupled with a shortage of motive power and a general lack of maintenance, led to a progressive deterioration in the railway and its rolling stock. This situation, was not, of course, unique to the ByR Co., and with the coming of peace consideration was given to the future of a national railway network seriously weakened as a result

Bridgend station *c*. 1910. *Lens of Sutton*

A pre-Grouping view of Bridgend station with a Barry train, hauled by a 'J' class 2-4-2T, standing in the Vale of Glamorgan bay on the left of picture. *Lens of Sutton*

of its contribution to the war effort. This resulted in the decision to proceed with the amalgamation of the various independent companies of South Wales with the GWR.

The continuation of Government control of the railways after the end of the war was clearly a cause of resentment to the ByR Directors, but they were also not happy at the prospect of their company being absorbed into a much larger undertaking: on 20th May, 1921 the Board resolved '... that the railways should be handed back to the companies with the same freedom to manage their own affairs as existed before the War ...' Government control ended on 15th August, 1921, and four days later, on 19th August, Royal Assent was given to Railways Act, which brought about the 'Grouping' of the railway companies of the United Kingdom into four large concerns. The ByR was granted the dignity of becoming a 'Constituent' of the 'Greater' GWR, but the VoGR, being in law an independent undertaking, acquired the lesser status of an 'Absorbed' company. This distinction also resulted in different dates of amalgamation with the GWR: that of the Barry Railway being 8th May, 1922, and the Vale of Glamorgan Railway, 1st July, 1922. However, in both cases the arrangements were backdated to take effect from 1st January, 1922. On 1st August, 1922 a final meeting of VoGR shareholders was held, and was officially informed that the company had been absorbed by the GWR.

The main line through Bridgend station in the early years of this century.

Lens of Sutton

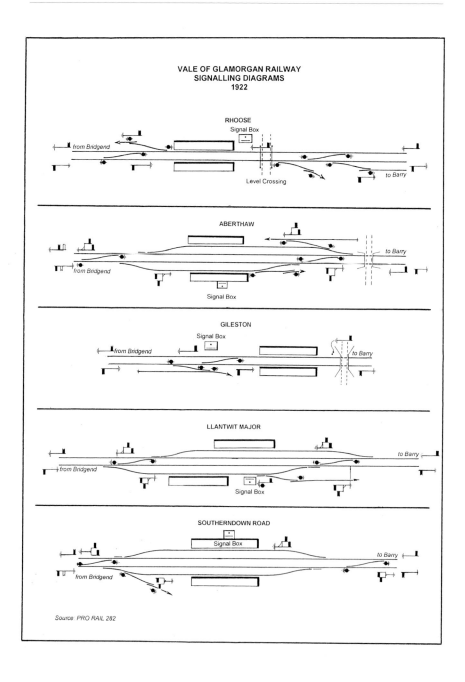

Chapter Seven

Under the Great Western

The world faced by railways, at the time of the Grouping, was very different to that which had existed before World War I. Costs had risen dramatically during and after the war, especially those of labour following the introduction of the 8 hour working day from 1st February, 1919. The war had also given a tremendous impetus to the development of the internal combustion engine and to road transport generally. This was heightened by the post-war disposal of surplus military vehicles, which were eagerly snapped up by budding bus and lorry operators, who themselves had often received their training in the armed forces. However, despite these profound changes in their competitive environment, railways continued to be very highly regulated, when compared with other forms of transport.

In South Wales the formerly independent local companies were cushioned to some extent by becoming part of a much larger concern. At first, changes were confined mainly to organisational structures and paint schemes, but gradually the new ownership began to make its mark. As far as the Vale of Glamorgan line was concerned, the first significant indications of the new regime came on 1st July, 1923, when 2nd class passenger accommodation was abolished, and exactly a year later when Aberthaw station acquired the suffix 'High Level' to distinguish it from the ex-TVR station, which now became 'Aberthaw (Low Level)'.

The amount of coal traffic passing over the VoG line closely matched the fortunes of the coal trade at Barry Docks. Barry's coal exports had declined from a peak of over 11 million tons in 1913 to 7 million tons in 1920, but by the end of 1922 there was a substantial recovery, with nearly 10 million tons being handled in that year. Traffic remained at about this level during the early 1920s, but the return to the Gold Standard in 1925, followed by the miners' strike and ensuing General Strike in 1926, seriously undermined the basis of the coal export trade and led directly to its subsequent decline. Nevertheless, this impact was not immediately apparent, and even in 1930 nearly 8 million tons of coal were exported from Barry Docks. However, during the 1930s the export trade went into a catastrophic decline, from which it was never to recover, and by 1940 annual shipments had fallen to just under 3½ million tons. Inevitably, this decline was matched by a progressive reduction in the number of coal trains passing over the Vale of Glamorgan line.

Local goods traffic, especially that worked over short distances, was especially vulnerable to the growth of road competition. The tonnages dealt with at Vale stations declined by 25 per cent between 1923 and 1933, but this picture is complicated by the inclusion of private siding traffic (especially that of Aberthaw and Rhoose cement works):

Top-left table

VALE OF GLAMORGAN BRANCH. — Down Trains — Week Days.

Time allowance for Freight Trains. See page 2.

Distances from Barry.	STATIONS.	Station No.	Ruling Gradient. 1 in
M C	**Barry**	7558	—
—	Barry Junction		—
1 44	Barry Sidings		—
2 62	Porthkerry		—
3 21	Porthkerry Lime Works		81 R
3 26	Rhoose		162 F
5 5	Aberthaw (High Level)		—
6 37	Aberthaw West		82 R
6 44	Gileston		85 R
9 56	Llantwit Major		103 F
15 7	Llandow Halt		141 F
16 74	Southerndown Road		—
18 36	Ewenny		100 R
19 16	Bridgend		—
19 16	Cowbridge Road Junction		—
	Cardiff Lime Works		—
	National Lime Co.		113 R
20 20	Coity Junction		—

Stations list (Down Trains, upper right and lower tables):

Barry
Barry Junction
Barry Sidings
Porthkerry
Porthkerry Lime Works
Rhoose
Aberthaw (High Level)
Aberthaw West
Gileston
Llantwit Major
Llandow Halt
Southerndown Road
Ewenny
Bridgend
Cowbridge Road Junction
National Lime Co.
Coity Junction

† From Cowbridge Road.

Great Western Railway Working Timetable for Vale of Glamorgan line, September 1928.

VALE OF GLAMORGAN BRANCH.

Down Trains. Week Days.

		H		B	B	B		Empties	Empties
		7.20 p.m. Grangetown to Llandilo Goods.		Passenger.	Passenger.	Passenger.		Empties.	
STATIONS.				SX	SO				
		P.M. dep.		P.M. 9 35 arr. dep.	P.M. dep. 10 39	P.M. arr. dep.		P.M. dep. 10 0	P.M. arr. dep. 10 50
Barry									
Barry Junction		7 58							
Barry Sidings		8 0	8 42					SUSPENDED	
Porthkerry									
Porthkerry Lime Works					10 38 10 39				
Rhoose				9 41	10 40 10 47				
Aberthaw (High Level)				9 47	10 47				
Aberthaw West		W		9 50 9 53	10 53				
Gileston				9 53					
Llantwit Major									
Llandow Halt									
Southerndown Road									
Ewenny									
Cowbridge Road Junction									
Bridgend		10 0 10 30						10 0	11 13 12 3	12 3
Cardiff Lime Works							B47	B40	
National Lime Co.									
Coity Junction									

Sundays.

STATIONS.		J	B	B	B	B	B	B
		9.10 a.m. Cardiff (General) Passenger.	Passenger.	Passenger.	Passenger.	8.0 p.m. Cardiff (General) Passenger.		
		A.M. dep.	A.M. 9 40 11 40 arr. dep.	P.M. 1 40 arr. dep.	P.M. 3 15 arr. dep.	P.M. 6 33 arr. dep.	P.M. 8 25 8 27 arr. dep.	
Barry								
Barry Junction		9 36	9 40	1 40	3 15	6 33	8 25 8 27	
Barry Sidings		1 50						
Porthkerry								
Porthkerry Lime Works								
Rhoose		9 48	9 49	1 48	3 23	6 41	8 35 8 36	
Aberthaw (High Level)		9 52	11 53	1 52	3 28	6 46	8 39 8 40	
Aberthaw West		9 57	11 58	1 57	3 33	6 50	8 44 8 45	
Gileston		10 4	12 4	2 4	3 40	6 57	8 51	
Llantwit Major			SUSPENDED	SUSPENDED			SUSPENDED	
Llandow Halt								
Southerndown Road								
Ewenny								
Cowbridge Road Junction								
Bridgend		3 3						
Cardiff Lime Works		B47						
National Lime Co.								
Coity Junction								

W—OR on Mondays only.

VALE OF GLAMORGAN BRANCH.

Down Trains. Week Days.

STATIONS.		B	B	K	B	B	A	B
		Passenger WSO	Passenger.	Goods.	Passenger. SX	12.57 p.m. Shrewsbury to Swansea Season Excursion. FO (July 13th to September 14th, inclusive.)	Passenger.	
		P.M. 1 35 arr. dep.	P.M. 2 50 arr. dep.	P.M. 3 5 arr. dep.	P.M. 4 15 arr. dep.	P.M. 4 58 arr. dep.	P.M. 5 2 arr. dep.	
Barry								
Barry Junction		1 30						
Barry Sidings			2 50					
Porthkerry				3 5				
Porthkerry Lime Works		1 41	2 58	3 25C	R 3 35	SUSPENDED	5 21	5 20 5 29
Rhoose		1 44	2 59 3 3		4 23 4 27		5 23	5 24 5 29
Aberthaw (High Level)		1 47	3 7		4 24			5 30
Aberthaw West		1 52 1 58	3 15		4 27			5 36
Gileston		1 58	3 23					
Llantwit Major			3 27					
Llandow Halt								
Southerndown Road								
Ewenny								
Cowbridge Road Junction								
Bridgend		3 36		4 20	4 35	5 58		
Cardiff Lime Works								
National Lime Co.				B29				
Coity Junction								

STATIONS.		B	J	A	MO	B	
		Passenger.	Empties	9.0 a.m. Penzance to Swansea Season Excursion. MO (July 9th to September 17th inclusive. August 6th excepted.)	Passenger.	Second trip of 3.5 p.m. ex Barry Sidings.	
		P.M. 6 18 arr. dep.	P.M. 6 30 dep.	P.M. 6 35 6 37 arr. dep.	P.M. 7 25 arr. dep.	P.M. 8 10 arr. dep.	
Barry							
Barry Junction		6 30	6 30	6 35	7 25		
Barry Sidings							
Porthkerry							
Porthkerry Lime Works		6 27		6 57		8 19	8 19 8 23
Rhoose		6 31				8 22	8 23
Aberthaw (High Level)		6 36				8 27	8 28
Aberthaw West		6 43				8 34	8 33 8 34
Gileston		6 51					
Llantwit Major		6 54		SUSPENDED			
Llandow Halt							
Southerndown Road							
Ewenny		7 4			7 30 7 33		
Cowbridge Road Junction							
Bridgend			6 43			8 38	
Cardiff Lime Works			B40			B29	
National Lime Co.							
Coity Junction							

Great Western Railway Working Timetable for Vale of Glamorgan line, September 1928.

VALE OF GLAMORGAN BRANCH.

Up Trains. — Week Days.

Distance from Bridgend	STATIONS.	Ruling Gradient	Time allowances for Freight Trains. See Page 2.										
			Vacuum and Express Trains.		Ordinary Goods.								
			Point to Point Times Express Train.	Point to Point Times Vac'm Train.	Allow for Stop.	Allow for Start.	Point to Point Times.	Allow for Stop.	Allow for Start.				

STATIONS.

Coity Junction
National Lime Co.
Cardiff Lime Works
Bridgend
Cowbridge Road Junction
Ewenny
Southerndown Road
Llandow Halt
Llanwit Major
Gileston
Aberthaw West
Aberthaw (High Level)
Rhoose
Porthkerry Lime Works
Stop Board
Barry Sidings
Barry Junction
Barry

† From Bridgend. 3, 3 and 4 mins. from Coity respectively. ‡ 8 mins. when stopping for water.

NOTE.—The Stop Board, Porthkerry Incline, is fixed on the Up side of the Up line between Porthkerry West and Barry Sidings, about 140 yards west of the 2 mile post.

VALE OF GLAMORGAN BRANCH.

Up Trains. — Week Days.

STATIONS.

Coity Junction
National Lime Co.
Cardiff Lime Works
Bridgend
Cowbridge Road Junction
Ewenny
Southerndown Road
Llandow Halt
Llanwit Major
Gileston
Aberthaw West
Aberthaw (High Level)
Rhoose
Porthkerry Lime Works
Stop Board
Barry Sidings
Barry Junction
Barry

Great Western Railway Working Timetable for Vale of Glamorgan line, September 1928.

VALE OF GLAMORGAN BRANCH.

Up Trains. Week Days.

STATIONS.	Passenger. SX		Passenger.			Return 2.5 p.m. ex Barry Sidings.	MO Cattle RR	Passenger.			Goods	Passenger.		
	arr. P.M.	dep. P.M.	arr. P.M.	dep.		dep. P.M.	P.M.	arr. P.M	dep. P.M.		dep. P.M.	arr. P.M.	dep. P.M.	
Coity Junction														
National Lime Co.														
Cardiff Lime Works			4 36			4 0								
Bridgend				4 44										
Cowbridge Road Junction			4 43	4 49			5 13		5 45	5 52	5 5		7 53	7 54	
Ewenny			4 46	4 57									7 58	7 59	
Southerndown Road			4 56	6 4									8 7	
Llandow Halt		9 16	6 3					5 61	6 1			8 13	8 14	
Llantwit Major		9 22						6 56	6 1					
Gileston	9 21		6 7	6 12		5 20	5 P⁴⁴	5 57	6 2					
Aberthaw West	9 25		6 12	6 13	5 20	4 58						8 18	8 19	
Aberthaw (High Level)	9 30										8 23	8 24	
Rhoose		9 31												
Porthkerry Lime Works										6 36				
Stop Board										6 53				
Barry Sidings						5 12	5 55							
Barry Junction														
Barry	9 38		5 20		B 35	B 47	5 55		6 9		B 29		8 30	

Up Trains. Week Days. (continued)

STATIONS.	Passenger.			Return 6.30 p.m. ex Barry Sidings.		6.30 p.m. Llandilo Jc. to Penarth Junction Goods. V		Light Eng. line. SX		Light Eng. gine. SO		Return 10.0 a.m. ex Barry Sidings.	
	arr. P.M.	dep. P.M.		dep. P.M.		arr. P.M.	dep. P.M.	dep. P.M.		dep.		dep. P.M.	
Coity Junction													
National Lime Co.													
Cardiff Lime Works						10 42	10 50						
Bridgend											11 55	
Cowbridge Road Junction				8 60 10								
Ewenny												
Southerndown Road								10⅒	10⅒			
Llandow Halt		9 15										
Llantwit Major		9 22				11 58 P12 1	12 20				1 P13	
Gileston	9 21					12 16 12 20	12 22				1 27	
Aberthaw West	9 25											
Aberthaw (High Level)	9 30									10⅗30		
Rhoose		9 31		10 28 10 43								
Porthkerry Lime Works												
Stop Board												
Barry Sidings				10P 8 10P28				10⅒	10⅒	10⅗30		
Barry Junction								11⅒35		11⅒35		
Barry	9 38			B 40	B 39						B 47	

V—Temporarily diverted via Main Line.

VALE OF GLAMORGAN BRANCH.

Up Trains. Sundays.

STATIONS.	Return 10.50 p.m. Barry Sidings Goods. (Sats.)		Passenger. B		Passenger. B		Passenger. B		Passenger. B	
	dep.		arr. A.M.	dep. A.M.	arr. P.M.	dep. P.M.	arr. P.M.	dep. P.M.	arr. P.M.	dep. P.M.
Coity Junction										
National Lime Co.										
Cardiff Lime Works										
Bridgend	3 50								2 30	2 37
Cowbridge Road Junction										
Ewenny										
Southerndown Road									2 41	
Llandow Halt			10 22	10 29	12 56	12 57			2 40	2 46
Llantwit Major										
Gileston			10 28	10 33		1 6	2 36			
Aberthaw West			10 37	10 38		1 5	2 45			
Aberthaw (High Level)	4 P16 5 12									
Rhoose	4 P38									
Porthkerry Lime Works	2 3 P2 8									
Stop Board	2 22									
Barry Sidings										
Barry Junction										
Barry	B 47		10 45		1 13		2 53			

Up Trains. Sundays. (continued)

STATIONS.	Passenger.		Cardiff (General) Passenger. B		Cardiff (Queen St.) Passenger. B	
	arr. P.M.	dep. P.M.	arr. P.M.	dep. P.M.	arr. P.M.	dep. P.M.
Coity Junction						
National Lime Co.						
Cardiff Lime Works						
Bridgend						
Cowbridge Road Junction						
Ewenny						
Southerndown Road						
Llandow Halt			7 20 7 27		9 15 9 22	
Llantwit Major	4 36	4 30 4 37				
Gileston			7 26	7 30	9 21	9 25 9 30
Aberthaw West	4 40	4 41	7 30 7 35	7 31 7 36	9 26 9 31	
Aberthaw (High Level)	4 45	4 46				
Rhoose						
Porthkerry Lime Works						
Stop Board						
Barry Sidings						
Barry Junction						
Barry	4 53		7 43 7 50		9 38 9 43	

Great Western Railway Working Timetable for Vale of Glamorgan line, September 1928.

An ex-Barry Railway class 'B1' 0-6-2T GWR No. 273 (ByR No. 122) at the western end of the down platform at Llantwit Major, having left a very short local goods on the down main, c. 1935.

W. John Collection

Llandow Halt with its ex-Barry Railway signals and elevated signal box, c. 1935.

R.P. Griffiths

	1923	*1933*
Southerndown Road	44,385 tons	35,844 tons
Llantwit Major	10,891 tons	3,203 tons
Gileston	2,950 tons	577 tons
Aberthaw	164,675 tons	141,226 tons
Rhoose	111,310 tons	70,209 tons

Livestock was an important item in 1923, with a total of 1,038 wagons handled at Vale stations, of which no less than 980 were dealt with at Llantwit Major alone. The scale of the traffic at this station was such that it merited special mention in the GWR Working Timetable:

> The shunting at Llantwit Major will be performed by a horse when the number of cattle wagons permit of this being done. When a special engine is required for the work the Llantwit Major station master will be responsible for ordering an engine and van from Barry in good time.

This traffic gradually declined during the 1920s and early 1930s, but as late as 1936 Llantwit Major was still handling an annual total in excess of 400 wagons. However, the following year saw the collapse of the trade, with only 55 cattle wagons recorded, with the total falling again in 1938 to only 31 wagons.

The inter-war years saw the development of comprehensive networks of bus services in rural areas, and the Vale of Glamorgan was no exception in this regard. The 1920s were a period of rapid growth, with consolidation being the principal feature of the 1930s. It will be recalled that a motor bus service had been introduced between Bridgend and Southerndown in January 1915, but it was not until 1923 that competitive bus services appeared along the main Barry-Llantwit Major-Bridgend corridor. Generally speaking, such services tended to divide this corridor into two sections: Barry-Llantwit Major, and Llantwit Major-Bridgend. Coincidently, 1923 saw the introduction of bus services on both of these sections. In February H.H. Gosling of Wick commenced operating as 'Vale Motor Services' on the Bridgend - Ogmore-by-Sea - Llantwit Major route, while that December J.H. Hill introduced a Barry-Llantwit Major service. In January 1924 Griffiths Bros started up between Barry and Rhoose, and by May 1926 buses belonging to T. White were also running between Barry and Llantwit Major. In March 1928 South Wales Commercial Motors (SWCM) introduced a Penarth-Barry-Llantwit Major-Bridgend service. The SWCM had been formed in 1920, and had gone on to establish a strong base in Bridgend. In 1929 the company, together with a number of other operators, was combined with the road passenger services of the GWR to form the Western Welsh Omnibus Co. (WWO), with the GWR holding a 50 per cent stake in the new undertaking, the arrangement coming into effect on 1st April of that year.

This period of rapid expansion was followed by one of consolidation. The first example of this occurred on the Bridgend-Llantwit Major route, when, in November 1933, Vale Motor Services combined with Thomas & Son of St Brides Major (who had previously operated on the Bridgend-Southerndown route) to form 'Green & White Services Ltd'. The new company worked the Bridgend-Wick-Llantwit Major and Bridgend-Southerndown-St Brides Major routes.

BRIDGEND AND BARRY.

Week Days.

Miles		a.m.	a.m.	a.m.	a.m.	a.m.	p.m.		p.m.	p.m.			p.m.	p.m.	p.m.	p.m.	p.m.	Sundays. a.m.	p.m.	p.m.	p.m.	p.m.	p.m.
	Bridgend . . . . dep.			8 32	9 46	11 30			1 53				4 47		7 40	9 50							
4	Southerndown Road . . . ,,				9 54	11 38			2 1				4 55		7 49	9 58							
5¾	Llandow Halt . . . . ,,				9 59	11 43			2 6				5 0		7 53	9 33							
9¼	Llantwit Major . . . ,,	6 28	8 15		10 6	11 50	12 25		2 13	3 10			5 7	5 53	8 0	9 40	10 22	12 50	2 30	4 30	7 25	9 25
12¼	Gileston for St.Athan & The Leys ,,	6 36	8 21		10 12	11 56	12 31		2 19	3 16			5 13	5 59	8 6	9 46	10 29	12 57	2 37	4 37	7 32	9 32
14	Aberthaw (High Level) . . ,,	6 40	8 25		10 16	12 0	12 35		2 23	3 20		4 53	5 17	6 3	8 10	9 50	10 33	1 1	2 41	4 41	7 36	9 36
16¼	Rhoose . . . . ,,	6 44	8 29		10 21	12 5	12 39		2 28	3 24		4 45	5 22	6 7	8 15	9 55	10 38	1 6	2 46	4 46	7 41	9 41
19	Barry . . . . arr.	6 52	8 37	9 4	10 28	12 12	12 47		2 35	3 32		4 50	5 29	6 15	8 23	10 3	10 45	1 13	2 53	4 53	7 48	9 48

		a.m.	a.m.	a.m.	a.m.		p.m.	p.m.	p.m.	p.m.	p.m.	p.m.	p.m.	p.m.		p.m.	a.m.	a.m.	p.m.	p.m.	p.m.	p.m.
	Barry . . . . dep	5 50	8 0	10 7	11 45		12 40	1 35	5 14	6 15	7 25	8 10	9 33		10 50	9 48	11 40	1 40	3 15	6 33	8 27
	Rhoose . . . . ,,	5 59	8 9	10 15	11 50		12 48	1 43	4 23	5 22	6 23		8 18	9 46		10 55	9 57	11 49	1 49	3 24	6 42	8 36
	Aberthaw (High Level) . ,,	6 3	8 13	10 19	11 54		12 52	1 47	3 4	4 26	5 26	6 27		8 22	9 50	10 45	10 1	11 53	1 53	3 25	6 46	8 40
	Gileston for St.Athan & The Leys ,,	6 8	8 18	10 23	11 58		1	1 51	3 8		5 30	6 31		8 26	9 54	10 46	10 6	11 58	1 58	3 33	6 51	8 45
	Llantwit Major . . . ,,	6 14	8 26	10 31	12 5		1 4	1 58	3 16		5 37	6 39		8 34	10 1	10 52	10 12	12 4	2 4	3 39	6 57	8 51
	Llandow Halt . . . ,,		8 34	10 39			1 12			3 24		6 47		8 42								
	Southerndown Road . . ,,		8 38	10 43			1 16			3 28		6 51		8 46		Sata.						
	Bridgend . . . . arr.		8 48	10 51			1 24			3 36		6 59	7 55	8 54		only						

W—On Wednesdays and Saturdays runs 8 minutes later throughout.

Great Western Railway public timetable for the Vale of Glamorgan line, 18th July-11th September, 1932.

The remainder of the 1930s saw the progressive takeover of the smaller local concerns by WWO Co. The first to be absorbed was T. White, which was leased to the WWO Co. in December 1935, before being acquired in December of the following year. Green & White was bought up in April 1937, but continued to operate in independent guise until February 1938. Finally in November 1938 J.H. Hill was purchased by WWO Co., giving that company a monopoly on the Bridgend - Llantwit Major - Barry corridor.

A number of other minor operators had also appeared on parts of the main routes, but all had gone by 1935. In addition to services along the Barry-Bridgend corridor, other routes operated between Cowbridge and Llantwit Major, and, from 22nd February, 1937, Cowbridge and St Athan.

Growing competition from bus services and increasing car ownership had a dramatic effect on passenger traffic on the VoG line, with the number of tickets sold at stations falling by over 50 per cent between 1923 and 1933. Decline was steepest in the 1920s, with a much more gradual fall during the early and middle 1930s. Rates of decline at individual station varied greatly, with the biggest loss over the period being at Aberthaw, which in 1933 had only 20 per cent of its 1923 ticket sales, whilst somewhat paradoxically, considering its isolated location, Southerndown Road retained nearly 70 per cent of its 1923 total.

	Tickets sold	
	1923	1933
Southerndown Road	6,168	4,225
Llantwit Major	25,339	15,034
Gileston	15,518	5,584
Aberthaw	21,103	4,205
Rhoose	32,261	16,036
Total	100,389	45,084

Nevertheless, with the exception of Southerndown Road, the Vale stations were all relatively well-placed for the settlements they purported to serve, and the railway itself followed the main flow of demand to Barry and Cardiff. Indeed, it was to retain a virtual monopoly of public transport to Cardiff until the end of the passenger service in 1964. Thus the decline in passenger traffic, although marked, was nowhere near as bad as on some other local lines in South Wales, where reductions of 90 per cent in ticket sales, over the above period, were not uncommon. As a comparison, tickets sold at Cowbridge station fell from 66,140 in 1923 to only 5,349 in 1933.

One casualty of this period of increased costs and declining traffic was the ex-TVR passenger train service between Cowbridge and Aberthaw (Low Level), which was withdrawn on 5th May, 1930. However, this made very little difference to the passenger traffic of the VoG line, as, in later years, very few passengers had made the long trudge between the two stations at Aberthaw. Aberthaw (Low Level) was closed to goods traffic on 1st November, 1932, thereby making redundant the suffix 'High Level' at the surviving station.

With the decline in traffic after the Grouping, staffing levels at Vale stations were also reduced, although not in proportion to the loss of business experienced. Overall, staffing fell by 25 per cent in the decade after the Grouping, but at Llantwit Major the number of staff fell from 14 to 10 over this period.

In spite of this decline there was little of the reduction in facilities which was to become such a depressing feature of later years. The most significant loss came on 11th October, 1930, when the down relief line between Porthkerry and Rhoose was converted into a down siding, worked from Rhoose. In addition, a number of the private sidings serving the smaller lime works and quarries were taken out of use. Elsewhere, other sidings remained in use despite the increasing role of road transport.

Perhaps because of the unrelating gloom of the Depression years and the international unease, one event involving the VoG line seems to have attracted more attention than otherwise might have been the case. In November 1936, King Edward VIII undertook a tour of the valley communities of South Wales, in which he was moved, on account of the poverty he witnessed, to remark that 'something must be done'. This tour commenced on Wednesday 18th November, 1936, when the King left Paddington by train at 12.55 am. At His Majesty's request, ordinary rolling stock was employed, the train consisting of six coaches, including two first class sleeping cars, hauled by 'Castle' class 4-6-0 No. 5056 *Ogmore Castle*.

The train ran non-stop through the night to Llantwit Major, where it arrived at 5.35 am. It was then berthed in the goods sidings behind the station. After breakfast, the King left by the goods yard entrance, across which had been hung banners, flags and bunting, and passed through streets packed with enthusiastic well-wishers to his first engagement at nearby Boverton, where he was to inspect houses built for the Welsh Land Settlement Scheme. From there he went on to tour the coalfield valleys by road.

The 'Royal Train', meanwhile, was taken by a 2-6-2T of class '41XX' to Cardiff for cleaning, gassing and watering, before being worked to Mountain Ash (Cardiff Road) station, where the King was to rejoin it after the first day of his tour. After visiting Usk, Cwmbran and Rhymney, the Royal party returned to Paddington at 3.45 pm on Friday, 20th November, 1936, arriving at 7.10 that evening.

The 'Royal Train', hauled by '51XX' 2-6-2T, prepares to depart for Cardiff, having deposited King Edward VIII at Llantwit Major on 13th November, 1936.   *W. John Collection*

GWR 'Manor' class 4-6-0 No. 7811 *Dunley Manor* leaves Porthkerry tunnel with LNER stock on the Newcastle-Swansea express *c.* 1935.   *J. Hubback, courtesy John Hodge*

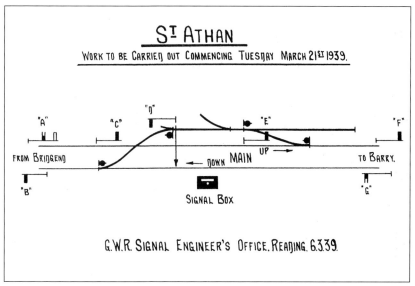

Great Western Railway: St Athan signalling diagram 1939.

Whilst coal traffic over the VoG line continued its remorseless decline, the late 1930s saw a substantial upturn in local goods and passenger traffic. The impetus for this came from the development of a major RAF air base at St Athan. To serve the new airfield a private siding was constructed from the Vale of Glamorgan line midway between Gileston and Llantwit Major, under an agreement with the Secretary of State for Air, dated 27th June, 1938. The new siding connection, controlled by a new signal box, named 'St Athan', was brought into use on 21st March, 1939. The nearest passenger station was at Gileston, but although this was reasonably placed for the eastern part of the RAF camp, the western part was poorly served. To remedy this deficiency a new halt, called 'St Athan', even though it was about two miles from that village, was opened on 1st September, 1939, just east of the junction with the RAF siding.

The development of RAF St Athan led to a significant growth in business at Llantwit Major and Gileston stations. The decline in their ticket sales was reversed, with tickets sold increasing, between 1936 and 1938, from 14,490 to 21,268 at Llantwit Major, and from 6,286 to 34,680 at Gileston. Whilst this occurred during the construction phase, the opening of the air base brought with it a continuing need for the transport of service and civilian personel which helped sustain the recovery in passenger traffic. Other stations on the line, with the exception of Southerndown Road, also shared in this upturn.

Llantwit Major also saw a substantial increase in its goods traffic, associated with the development of the airfield, with the total handled rising from 4,020 tons in 1936 to 37,804 tons in 1938. Staffing at the station increased from 8 to 14 over this period, and in 1938 a new 20 ton weighing machine replaced the old cart weighbridge in the goods yard.

At the Bridgend end of the line, re-armament in the years leading up to World War II saw the building of two major ordnance depots. That at Tremains, to the east of Bridgend, was alongside and served off the South Wales main line, but was also connected, by a short curve, to the VoG line, near Cowbridge Road Junction. The other, at Brackla Hill, to the east of Bridgend, was connected by a single track siding to a triangular junction with the down line of the Coity loop. To cater for these sidings a radical reorganisation of the lines between Coity Sidings and Cowbridge Road Junction was brought into use on 19th May, 1938. The up line between these points (18 m. 56 ch. to 19 m. 47 ch.) was converted into a siding for use by the War Department, whilst the former down line became the up and down running line.

The war years also saw a substantial increase in the amount of freight passing over the VoG line, with traffic from the various military sidings augmented by that diverted off the busy South Wales main line. In addition, the cement works at Rhoose and Aberthaw saw substantially increased output, with much of it being shipped at Barry. There was also a Naval Victualling Depot at Barry from where a heavy traffic was dispatched to other South Wales ports. From 1942 United States Forces started handling considerable quantities of equipment and stores through Barry Docks, which were to play an important part in the run up to D-Day.

Passenger traffic continued to benefit from the presence of the RAF base at St Athan. Reflecting its growing importance, St Athan Halt was upgraded to the status of a station on 3rd May, 1943, although it continued to be referred to as 'The Halt' by older local people right up to closure in 1964. The number of passengers dealt with at Gileston was such as to justify the building of a large canopy on the up platform. On 19th April, 1943 Llandow (Wick Road) Halt, midway between Llantwit Major and Llandow Halt, opened to serve the nearby RAF Llandow air base.

Following the end of hostilities the lines between Coity Sidings and Cowbridge Road Junction were restored to their former status as up and down mineral lines (by 5th May, 1948).

For the railways the immediate post-war years were dominated by the after-effects of the contribution they had made to the war effort and by various shortages. The Transport Act of 1947 brought about the nationalisation of the country's rail network, and from 1st January, 1948 the VoG line became part of the Western Region of British Railways.

Chapter Eight

The British Railways Era

Nationalisation did not bring any immediate changes of significance to the Vale of Glamorgan line. Once again, paint schemes and signposting were altered to reflect the new ownership, but otherwise things continued much as before. However, the outside world was changing fast, presenting fresh challenges, but also bringing great dangers for the future of railways such as the VoG line.

For freight traffic, particularly the conveyance of coal to Barry Docks, prospects for the railway were not encouraging. By 1950 only 2,400,000 tons of coal were handled at the docks, with the decline continuing through the next decade to only 600,000 tons in 1960. This was accompanied by a further gradual reduction in the number of coal trains passing over the VoG line to the docks. During the same period imports through Barry assumed a much greater importance, doubling from 300,000 tons between 1950 and 1960, but here road transport was to play an increasingly important role. In any event, much of this new business was destined for places to the east of Barry and so was of no benefit to the VoG line. Local goods traffic also declined in the face of increasing road competition, particularly after the train drivers' strike of 1955.

This picture of general decline was dramatically changed by a development alongside the VoG line, undertaken by another nationalised industry, which was eventually to produce traffic flows for the railway far in excess of the highest achieved in the glory days of the coal export trade. In the early 1950s the need for additional electricity generating capacity in South Wales was recognised, and in 1953 plans were prepared for a new power station of advanced design, with six 100,000 kw units. The site chosen for this new facility was at The Leys, the small peninsular to the west of the mouth of the River Thaw at Aberthaw. Planning permission for the new power station, which was to be on the site of a golf course, was granted on 3rd November, 1955, with construction starting during the following year. A sea wall, 1¼ miles long, was built, together with a cooling water caisson, about ½ mile offshore, linked to the generators by a tunnel under the sea bed. The first generating unit was brought into use on 7th February, 1960, with the last of the six producing its first power on 18th August, 1963.

To reach the new generating station a branch line, about 1¾ miles long, was constructed from a junction with the VoG line, just east of Aberthaw station. Two reception sidings were provided on the branch, close to this junction, together with a single track connection from the western end of these sidings to join the VoG line at Aberthaw West. Initially, only a single track was laid over the power station branch. This made a trailing connection to the up line at Aberthaw, and it was not until 23rd July, 1961, some time after the commencement of coal traffic, that the fully signalled junction and that at Aberthaw West were brought into use, by which time the branch itself had been doubled.

Ex-Barry Railway 'B1' class 0-6-2T No. 271 (ByR No. 115) leaves Coity Sidings with a mineral train bound for Barry on 6th March, 1948. At this date the former up line between Coity Sidings and Cowbridge Road Junction was used for up and down traffic, with the former down line retained as a siding by the War Department. *Ian L. Wright*

'Castle' class 4-6-0 No. 5072 *Hurricane* hauls a diverted express through Porthkerry Park in 1954. *R.O. Tuck*

BR Standard 2-6-2T No. 82039 leaves Bridgend on the 1.50 pm to Barry on 4th July, 1955.
S. Rickard Collection/Copyright B.J. Miller

Standard class 2-6-2T No. 82044 leaves Gileston with the 2.53 pm Barry-Bridgend on 18th April, 1957. *S. Rickard Collection/Copyright B.J. Miller*

A general view of Barry station on 29th August, 1958, with the 3.00 pm (SX) Llantwit Major-Barry and 2.46 pm Cardiff-Barry.   *S. Rickard Collection/Copyright B.J. Miller*

'Britannia' class 4-6-2 No. 70020 passes the new Junction of the Aberthaw Power Station branch with a diverted express in 1957. At this date access to the branch was controlled by a ground frame situated at the junction itself.   *R.O. Tuck*

'County' class 4-6-0 No. 1001 *County of Bucks* approaches Aberthaw station with a diverted express from the west in 1957. *R.O. Tuck*

'Castle' class 4-6-0 No. 4081 *Warwick Castle* with a diverted express runs through Aberthaw on the down main in 1957. *R.O. Tuck*

A wet day at Bridgend with 'Castle' class 4-6-0 No. 7003 *Elmley Castle* arriving on a down express on 27th July, 1958. Note the station nameboard still refers to the 'Vale of Glamorgan Railway'.   *Michael Hale*

Bridgend station with an up main line train and two trains in the Bridgend Valleys bay, 1st August, 1958.   *Michael Hale*

The opening of the Aberthaw Power Station gave a much needed boost to the freight traffic of the VoG line. This was particularly welcome at a time when the coal export trade had all but faded away. In 1963 Barry and Swansea were designated as the sole exporting ports for coal in South Wales, but this brought only temporary respite on the long road of decline. Most of the new traffic attracted by the power station came from the Barry direction, however, as shown by the British Railways Traffic Densities Map of July 1962, which showed the Bridgend-Aberthaw section carrying only 5,000-10,000 tons of freight per week, compared with the Aberthaw-Barry total of over 50,000 tons.

Passenger traffic had remained at a high level following the increase which had occurred during the war years. In the early 1950s the VoG line was generating more revenue than either the Aberdare or Maerdy branches, both of which served far more populous districts. However, the 1950s also saw a resumption in the growth of car ownership and usage after the end of petrol rationing and other restrictions of the War years and the immediate post-war period. At the same time, local bus services remained very popular, especially for shorter journeys. Although the VoG line retained its supremacy for Cardiff traffic, this was undermined by the need to change trains at Barry on most services. Where through trains were provided this was usually at the expense of a time-consuming detour via Penarth. As a result of these factors there was a gradual decline in the patronage of Vale passenger trains, although the line still saw busy periods, particularly on Saturdays. The introduction of diesel multiple units (dmu) in 1958 stemmed the tide for a while, but the early 1960s were not an encouraging time for local train services. A portent of things to come occurred on 23rd October, 1961, with the complete closure of Southerndown Road station. By 18th June, 1962, when the frequency of the passenger train service was drastically reduced and the Sunday service withdrawn, the future of the line was clear for all to see.

The BR Traffic Densities Map of July 1962 showed the Aberthaw-Barry section of the VoG Line carrying 5,000-10,000 passengers per week, with the line to the west of Aberthaw seeing less than 5,000. In fact the real dividing point was at Llantwit Major, the section onwards to Bridgend having long been very poorly patronised. It came as no surprise, therefore, when 'Barry-Bridgend' appeared in the schedule of passenger services to be withdrawn which was appended to the document *The Reshaping of British Railways* (otherwise known as the 'Beeching Report'), made public in March 1963. Little time was lost in publishing proposals for the withdrawal of the passenger train service over the VoG line. Having considered various objections, the Transport Users' Consultative Committee recommended that the proposals be approved, subject to the provision of certain additional bus services. This was accepted by the Minister of Transport, and the date for the withdrawal of the service was fixed for Monday 15th June, 1964.

As there was no Sunday service the last local passenger trains ran over the VoG line on Saturday 13th June, 1964. On the Llantwit Major to Bridgend section, the last timetabled working was the 7.41 pm from Bridgend, whilst the last train to leave Llantwit Major for Barry was at 10.00 pm. Trains terminating at Llantwit Major usually departed for Barry from the platform at which they

Table 129 — BRIDGEND and BARRY

Week Days

Miles		am U	am	am	am U	am U	am	pm S	pm SU	pm G	pm	pm E	pm S	pm	pm U
—	**Bridgend A** dep	..	..	..	..	9 53	11 9	..	..	..	1 40	..	3 10	..	4 25
4	Southerndown Road	..	..	..	..	10 2	1118	..	..	..	1 49	..	3 19	..	4 34
5¾	Llandow Halt	..	..	..	..	10 6	1123	..	..	..	1 54	..	3 24	..	4 39
7¼	Llandow (Wick Road)	..	..	..	..	1011	1127	..	..	..	1 58	..	3 28	..	4 43
9¼	Llantwit Major	6 18	..	7 0	8 3	1016	1132	1222	1254	1 33	2 3	3 0	3 33	4 25	4 50
10½	St. Athan	6 22	..	7 4	8 6	1020	1136	1226	1258	1 37	2 8	3 4	3 38	4 29	4 55
12½	Gileston	6 27	..	7 9	8 11	1025	1140	1230	1 3	1 42	2 12	3 9	3 42	4 34	4 59
14	Aberthaw	6 30	..	7 13	8 15	1028	1144	1234	1 7	1 46	2 16	3 13	3 46	4 38	5 3
15¾	Rhoose	6 35	7 5	7 18	8 19	1032	1150	1239	1 11	1 50	2 20	3 17	3 50	4 43	5 7
19	**Barry** arr	6 44	7 13	7 26	8 27	1040	1158	1247	1 19	1 58	2 29	3 25	3 59	4 51	5 15

Week Days—continued / Sundays

	WD pm U	WD pm	WD pm	WD pm	WD pm E	WD pm S	WD pm V	WD pm S	Sun am U	Sun am	Sun pm	Sun pm U	Sun pm	Sun pm U	Sun pm U
Bridgend A dep	..	..	7 40	..	..	..	1025	1118	..	..	..	..	..	..	..
Southerndown Road	..	..	7 49	..	..	..	1034	1126	..	..	..	..	..	..	..
Llandow Halt	..	..	7 54	..	..	..	1039	1131	..	..	..	..	..	..	..
Llandow (Wick Road)	..	..	7 58	..	..	..	1043	1136	..	..	..	..	..	..	..
Llantwit Major	5 15	6 3	8 3	8 30	1025	1035	1050	1142	..	9 55	1255	2 25	5 23	6 18	8 55
St. Athan	5 19	6 7	8 8	8 34	1029	1039	1054	1145	..	9 59	1259	2 29	5 27	6 22	8 59
Gileston	5 24	6 12	8 12	8 39	1034	1044	1059	1150	..	10 4	1 4	2 34	5 32	6 27	9 4
Aberthaw	5 28	6 16	8 16	8 43	1038	1048	11 3	..	6 15	10 8	1 8	2 38	5 36	6 31	9 8
Rhoose	5 32	6 20	8 20	8 47	1042	1052	11 7	..	6 20	1012	1 12	2 42	5 40	6 35	9 12
Barry arr	5 40	6 28	8 29	8 55	1050	11 0	1115	12 5	6 28	1020	1 20	2 50	5 48	6 43	9 20

Week Days

Miles		am U	am	am U	am U	am U	am	am S	pm S	pm	pm G	pm E	pm S	pm	pm	pm	pm U	pm U	pm	pm
—	**Barry** dep	5 43	6 25	6 49	7 20	7 58	1010	1142	1215	1240	1255	1 50	2 8	2 53	3 42	4 44	5 27	6 22	7 42	9 10
3¼	Rhoose	5 51	6 33	6 57	7 28	8 6	1018	1150	1223	1248	1 3	1 58	2 16	3 1	3 50	4 52	5 35	6 30	7 50	9 18
5	Aberthaw	5 56	6 38	..	7 32	8 10	1022	1154	1225	1253	1 8	2 3	2 21	3 6	3 55	4 57	5 40	6 35	7 55	9 23
6½	Gileston	6 0	6 42	..	7 36	8 14	1026	1158	1232	1257	1 12	2 7	2 25	3 10	3 59	5 1	5 44	6 39	7 59	9 27
8½	St. Athan	6 4	6 46	..	7 41	8 19	1031	12 3	1236	1 1	1 16	2 11	2 29	3 14	4 3	5 5	5 48	6 43	8 3	9 31
9¾	Llantwit Major	6 9	6 51	..	7 45	8 24	1035	12 8	1241	1 6	1 21	2 16	2 34	3 19	4 8	5 10	5 53	6 48	8 8	9 36
11¾	Llandow (Wick Road)	..	..	..	..	8 30	1040	..	..	1 11	..	..	2 39	3 24	..	..	..	6 53	..	9 41
13¼	Llandow Halt	..	..	..	..	8 34	1044	..	..	1 15	..	..	2 42	3 28	..	..	..	6 57	..	9 45
15	Southerndown Road	..	..	..	..	8 38	1049	..	..	1 19	..	..	2 47	3 32	..	..	..	7 0	..	9 49
19	**Bridgend A** arr	..	..	..	..	8 47	1053	..	..	1 28	..	..	2 56	3 41	..	..	..	7 10	..	9 58

Week Days—continued / Sundays

	WD pm EU	WD pm SU	WD pm U	WD pm SU	WD pm U	WD night SU	Sun am U	Sun am	Sun am	Sun pm	Sun pm	Sun pm	Sun pm U	Sun pm U	Sun pm U
Barry dep	9 53	10 0	1048	1130	1158	1234	5 45	9 10	1140	1 35	3 55	5 40	8 12	1054	1145
Rhoose	10 1	10 8	1056	1138	12 6	..	5 53	9 18	1148	1 43	4 3	5 48	8 20	11 4	1152
Aberthaw	10 6	1012	11 0	1143	1211	..	5 58	9 23	1153	1 48	4 8	5 53	8 25	11 9	1157
Gileston	1010	1017	11 5	1145	1215	1250	..	9 27	1157	1 52	4 12	5 57	8 29	1113	12 1
St. Athan	1014	1021	11 9	1149	1219	1254	..	9 31	12 1	1 56	4 16	6 1	8 33	1117	12 6
Llantwit Major	1019	1026	1114	1154	1224	1259	..	9 36	12 6	2 1	4 21	6 6	8 38	1122	1211
Llandow (Wick Road)	..	..	..	..	..	..	..	..	..	..	..	..	..	..	..
Llandow Halt	..	..	..	..	..	..	..	..	..	..	..	..	..	..	..
Southerndown Road	..	..	..	..	..	..	..	..	..	..	..	..	..	..	..
Bridgend A arr	..	..	..	..	..	..	..	..	..	..	..	..	..	..	..

A "Western Welsh" omnibuses run between Bridgend, Ogmore-by-Sea and Southerndown. **E** Except Saturdays. **G** Fridays and Saturdays. **S** or S Saturdays only **U** Through Train to or from Cardiff (Table 125). **V** On Saturdays Through Train to Cardiff.

British Railways (Western Region) public timetable for the Vale of Glamorgan line, 9th June-14th September, 1958, following the introduction of diesel multiple units.

A 2-car dmu (later class '116') passes Rhoose Cement Works siding on a Barry-Llantwit Major working on 2nd July, 1960. *S. Rickard Collection/Copyright B.J. Miller*

had arrived, i.e. the down platform. Unusually, the last arrival from Barry, at
9.50 pm, ran forward, then reversed into the up platform. A small crowd, made
up, in the main, of local people, was there to see off the last train, which carried
only a few passengers. The atmosphere was subdued and there was none of the
absurd celebration which accompanied many last train departures. Instead
there was a genuine sense of impending loss. Amongst those in attendance was
Llantwit Major's last station master, Mr R. Everist, who had taken up his
appointment in June 1954, having moved from a similar post at Abergwynfi at
the head of the Afan Valley. Right on time, the final passenger train pulled out
of the station to blasts of the dmu's horn and explosions of fog detonators,
which had been placed, for some distance, along the up line. As the train
disappeared out of sight the spectators dispersed and made their way home.

As part of the closure arrangements a new 'express' bus service was
introduced between Llantwit Major and Cardiff, running at approximately
hourly intervals. Its route avoided Barry, which continued to be served by a
half-hourly service from Llantwit Major, but most services made a detour to
serve the village of St Athan and the adjoining RAF camp. Some buses took the
direct road via Wenvoe, whilst others turned off to serve Dinas Powis. The
average journey time for this service was about an hour, which was about the
same as that of the train service, which it replaced, but it always seemed much
longer. However, traffic congestion in Cardiff meant extended journey times in
the peak periods, when the through trains had completed the run between
Llantwit Major and the city centre in 55 minutes or less.

Llantwit Major station was host to one last passenger working on Friday 25th
June, 1965, when the Royal Train arrived at the disused down platform,
conveying the Queen and the Duke of Edinburgh, *en route* to an engagement at
Atlantic College, St Donats, about two miles to the west of the town. Later that
morning the Royal Party rejoined the train for the journey to Port Talbot, where
the Queen was to open the new Afan Lido. The station had been spruced up for
the occasion, provoking some controversy locally in view of British Rail's
continuing refusal to allow school excursions to be worked from Llantwit
Major.

The 1960s also witnessed the rundown and eventual elimination of goods
stations between Barry and Bridgend. Some, such as Southerndown Road
(closed 23rd October, 1961) and Aberthaw (closed 1st October, 1963), had seen
little traffic for many years, but Gileston and Rhoose, which closed on 28th
September, 1964, had been busier. This left Llantwit Major as the only local
goods station between Barry and Bridgend. This yard was to enjoy something
of an Indian Summer, its traffic boosted by construction materials for the new
Aberthaw 'B' Power Station, with, on occasions, up to 100 wagons crammed into
its sidings. However, once this contract was completed, traffic fell back to a
small amount of domestic coal, and the goods yard was closed on 3rd July, 1967.

The withdrawal of the passenger train service and closure of goods yards was
accompanied by a general reduction in facilities along the line. By far the most
signficant was the complete closure of the goods-only link between Cowbridge
Road Junction and Coity Sidings, which took place on 15th June, 1964. The
goods yard at Coity was retained as the principal goods depot for Bridgend and

0-6-0PT No. 4610 takes water at Barry Sidings, whilst working the 2 pm Barry Sidings-Pengam goods. *S. Rickard Collection/Copyright B.J. Miller*

Hauled by an ex-GWR class '52XX' 2-8-0T and banked by a '72XX' class 2-8-2T, a coal train for Aberthaw Power Station leaves Barry Sidings in 1964. *Ian L. Wright*

the surrounding area, being reached via the Llynfi Valley line at Coity Junction.

Passing loops at stations were also taken out of use, with those at Southerndown Road going in September 1963, Aberthaw (up side only) in December 1966, and Llantwit Major in January 1969. Extensive reductions also took place at Barry in conjunction with the abandonment of Barry Sidings. The number of signal boxes on the line was also gradually reduced, leaving only Cowbridge Road, near Bridgend (where a new box had been provided in 1965), St Athan, Aberthaw and Rhoose by the end of the decade.

In the midst of this depressing catalogue of the aftermath of the Beeching Report came two developments which were to herald a vast increase of traffic on the VoG line. The first was the decision to build another power station at Aberthaw, and the second was the introduction of 'Merry-go-round' (mgr) coal trains to convey power station coal traffic. The two were of course inter-related as a generating station the size of Aberthaw 'B' required a revolution in the transport of coal by rail. A planning application to build the power station was submitted on 27th July, 1962, with consent being granted on 19th March, 1963. It was to be constructed alongside, but to a more advanced design and on a much greater scale than the old Aberthaw 'A' station. There were to be three generating units each with an output of 500 megawatts, and a total fuel consumption of 570 tonnes of coal per hour. In order to provide for mgr operation, the layout at the terminus of the power station branch railway was altered, with the old dead-end arrangement serving tipplers giving way to a reversing loop line which enabled complete mgr trains to unload without stopping. The first power from Aberthaw 'B' was supplied on 10th December, 1968. In 1970 the old 'A' station had two of its coal burning units converted to oil firing, bringing regular workings of bulk oil trains to the VoG line.

For a time traffic also flowed out from the power station complex. The vast quantity of pulverised fuel ash (PFA) produced in the generation of electricity found a market in major motorway construction projects. PFA had been tipped alongside the power stations, in what had been the mouth of the River Thaw. In 1970 a siding was opened to enable the material to be taken out by rail. From 1st April, 1970 four PFA trains per day were run from this siding to Puxton, near Weston-super-Mare, in connection with the M5 motorway contract. A further stage of this project, commencing 26th April, 1971, required the working of PFA trains to Highbridge in Somerset.

For other sources of freight traffic the 1970s were a period of mixed fortunes. The RAF siding at St Athan, latterly used only for infrequent block coal trains to supply the camp's boilers, was taken out of use on 7th May, 1973, the private siding agreement having been terminated on 31st March of that year. A far more positive, and rather unexpected, development was the opening of a branch line to serve the Ford Motor Co.'s new engine factory, near Bridgend. Parliamentary powers for the construction of this line were obtained under the British Railways Act 1978, and on 17th August, 1978 the Welsh Office awarded the project a grant of £1,114,000 towards the total cost of £2,300,000. The contract for the new railway was awarded to Brunswick Construction of Pontyclun, who started work in April 1979, the new connection to the VoG line being installed in September of that year. The total length of the new line was

nearly two miles, with three bridges, two over minor roads and one over the River Ewenni, and a level crossing over the A48 Cardiff-Bridgend road. A facing crossover was provided in the VoG line to enable trains to run directly into the branch from the Barry direction. To have worked the traffic via Bridgend would have entailed two reversals and operating problems crossing the busy South Wales main line, so although the branch was only about a mile from Bridgend, it brought new traffic to almost the whole length of the VoG line. The Fords Factory branch was formally opened on 15th January, 1980, with Stanley Williams, Vice-President, Ford Europe, and Albert Barnes, BR Divisional Manager for South Wales, on the footplate of the locomotive of the inaugural train.

At Aberthaw Cement Works new sidings, also partly funded by Government grant, were brought into use on 16th October, 1980, to facilitate the conversion of the works from oil to coal. A trial mgr train, hauled by two class '37' locomotives, ran from Brynlliw Colliery on 6th November, 1980, with the regular service commencing on 5th December of that year.

It will be recalled that an isolated fragment of the VoGR had been retained, from Coity Junction, to serve Coity goods yard after the closure of the rest of the mineral loop from Cowbridge Road Junction in June 1964. With the gradual elimination of wagonload traffic and local goods facilities throughout the national railway network, it was only a matter of time before this short link was also swept away. The last coal train was worked into the siding on 2nd November, 1983, with the empties being taken out on 22nd of that month, but offical closure of the goods depot did not take place until 18th December, 1983.

The VoG line has seen few physical developments during the 1990s, the most significant being the closure of Aberthaw 'A' power station in 1995. However, radical organisational changes at national level have had their impact on the local scene. The Railways Act 1993, which foreshadowed the privatisation of British Rail, introduced a split between infrastructure provision and train operation, with the creation of Railtrack and the train operating units from 1st April, 1994. From this date operational property, track, structures, signalling and stations were transferred from the British Railways Board to the new infrastructure company, which was floated on the Stock Exchange on 20th May, 1996. Three trainload freight companies were formed, including Transrail which worked mgr and other trains over the VoG line. However, this change proved short-lived as all three were sold to Winconsin Central on 24th February, 1996, the company subsequently adopting the title 'English Welsh and Scottish Railway' (EWSR). The passenger train units were franchised to private companies during the three years after 1994. As a result, the VoG line now sees the trains of four private operators, with EWSR on freight workings, and Great Western, Virgin Cross Country and South Wales and West (renamed 'Wales & West Railway' in September 1997) on diverted passenger train services.

Chapter Nine

Locomotive and Train Working

The passenger train service between Barry and Bridgend, inaugurated on 1st December, 1897, was not exactly lavish, with only four trains each way daily and no Sunday service, but it was anticipated that it would be improved for the summer season in 1898. The introduction of the emergency timetable of only three trains each way, following the failure of Porthkerry viaduct in January 1898, proved to be only a temporary setback to this ambition. With the opening of the Porthkerry loop line on 25th April, 1898 the service was restored to four trains each way, with that year's summer timetable seeing it increased to six each way, with three round trips on Sundays. However, this level of service was evidently slightly too ambitious, at least as far as weekdays were concerned, for the following summer saw it reduced to five trains each way, but with one extra round trip on Sundays. On 9th August, 1899 the ByR Traffic Committee agreed to run an additional evening train to Bridgend for the benefit of passengers off the steamer service at Barry Pier.

The reopening of Porthkerry viaduct to passenger traffic on 9th April, 1900 was accompanied by the introduction of what was to become a consistent feature of the timetable right through to the withdrawal of the passenger service in 1964: a through train to Cardiff in the morning, for what were later to be termed 'commuters'. The number of passenger trains over the line was also increased, with the summer timetable for 1900 showing eight trains each way between Barry and Bridgend. The morning through train to Cardiff, although welcome, was not sufficient to satisfy public demands that all trains should run through to Cardiff, thereby avoiding the need to change trains at Barry. This issue was addressed by the ByR General Manager, Richard Evans, in a report dated 28th February, 1902, and it is worth quoting from this document in order to appreciate the practical difficulties associated with such a seemingly simple alteration:

> This train (i.e. from Bridgend) would have to be stopped clear of the Barry station and the junction with the Island Railway. The engine and leading brake van would then have to be cut off and taken away for the Barry Island train to draw in.
> . . . The Island train, after stopping at Barry station platform to discharge the Barry passengers, would have to shunt back against the Vale train, which would be standing west of the platform. These two portions would form the Cardiff train, which would then have to be coupled up and brought forward into the platform, so as to discharge any passengers and luggage for Barry that would be in the Vale train, and load up any passengers and luggage for the direction of Cardiff. I should say that these operations would take quite 10 or 15 minutes. The Vale passengers would remain in the train during these operations and the Cardiff passengers from Barry Island would also have to remain in the Island train while it will be setting back for the Vale portion. The above arrangement explains the delay that will be caused to the up train. I will now give you an idea as to the alterations and delays that would be caused to the down train.
> On the arrival of the Cardiff down train at Barry station, the engine would have to be cut off, get clear and stand on the Island Railway, then the Vale engine, which would

Class 'G' 0-4-4T No. 66 at Barry Shed in pre-Grouping days. Sister engine No. 68 worked the
inaugural passenger train over the VoGR in 1897.   *Real Photographs*

Barry Railway class 'J' 2-4-2T No. 89 at Barry Shed.   *C.W. Harris Collection*

have to stand in readiness on the down Vale line, would have to push back, pick up its coaches and get away on the Vale line, and stand there till the Island engine pushes back, picks up the remainder of the Cardiff train and proceeds to the Island. The Vale train would then push back and the engine would leave its train to pick up another brake van while the passengers would be entering the train. These operations would take at least 15 minutes.

Mr Evans then went on to note that the Barry Island train would need to be strengthened for its return to Cardiff, and that the arrangements outlined could not be applied in the summer months as the accommodation on the Barry Island portion would be inadequate for the needs of the traffic. While Mr Evans's assessment of the problem was perfectly logical to the railway mind, it did little to stop the passengers complaining when they continued to have to change trains at Barry.

The inaugural passenger train on the VoGR was hauled by ByR engine No. 68 of the 'G' class of 0-4-4Ts. This class comprised four engines, two of which (Nos. 66 and 67) had been completed by Vulcan Foundry in August 1892, and two (Nos. 68 and 69) by Sharp, Stewart & Co. in March 1895. These engines were initially used on the Barry-Cardiff service, but, following the introduction of the 'J' class of locomotives in 1897-1899, they were generally to be found on Barry-Porth trains.

Vale passenger trains were more usually in the hands of 2-4-2T engines, of which the ByR had two classes: the 'C' class and the 'J' class. The 'C' class had consisted of four engines (Nos. 21, 22, 37 and 52), originally built as 2-4-0Ts by Sharp, Stewart & Co. in 1889 and 1890. Nos. 21 and 22 were rebuilt to 2-4-2T configuration in 1898, and at about the same time Nos. 37 and 52 (also converted to 2-4-2T type) were sold to the Port Talbot Railway. The class 'J' engines were larger and comprised a total of 11 engines (Nos. 86 to 91, and 94 to 98), built by Hudswell, Clarke and Sharp, Stewart between 1897 and 1899.

Passenger rolling stock owned by the ByR, at the time of the opening of the VoGR, was a mixture of four- and six-wheeled carriages built by a variety of companies, including the Metropolitan Carriage & Wagon Co. and the Gloucester Carriage & Wagon Co. In 1902 a typical Vale train was reported to consist of a brake van, 3rd class coach, composite coach, 3rd class coach and brake van.

The early years of this century saw a wave of enthusiasm in railway circles for self-propelled steam railcars. South Wales was a popular area for these vehicles, with the TVR and its locomotive superintendent, Tom Hurry Riches, leading the way. In January 1904 the ByR General Manager, Richard Evans, visited Stroud in Gloucestershire to see for himself the experimental steam railcar which the GWR had introduced between Stonehouse and Chalford. He was sufficiently impressed with what he saw to conclude that a car built on similar lines, but 'somewhat larger and slightly modified', would meet the requirements of the ByR for its Cardiff- Pontypridd, via St Fagans, service. This had been introduced on 7th June, 1897 in competition with that of the TVR between Cardiff and Pontypridd, but had not flourished, as had been hoped. The use of steam railcars would enable its running costs to be reduced significantly, and would also allow the company to respond to pressures for extra stopping places along the route.

Class 'J' 2-4-2T No. 88 at Barry Shed in Barry Railway days. *LCGB*

Running as GWR No. 1321, ex-Barry Railway class 'J' 2-4-2T (ByR No. 98) stands alongside Barry Station signal box in 1922. *Author's Collection*

However, while railcars could meet the entire requirements of the Cardiff-Pontypridd route there would be difficulties in using them on the Barry-Porth and VoGR services. It was hoped that any problems of overcrowding during the winter months could be overcome by attaching trailers to the cars, but both lines would have to be worked by locomotives and coaches in the busy summer months. Mr Evans reported that the GWR was building railcars of an improved design, and that the North Eastern Railway (NER) was constructing a petrol driven vehicle. He recommended, therefore, that the ByR should await further developments before deciding on the matter; in the meantime he thought that the GWR might be prepared to lend the company a car for trial purposes. However, the ByR Traffic Committee was not prepared to exercise this degree of caution, and, on 4th February, 1904, the company's Locomotive Superintendent, J.H. Hosgood, was instructed to prepare a drawing for a steam 'motor car' (as they were generally known in South Wales).

Later that month Richard Evans, accompanied by J.H. Hosgood and William Waddell, the ByR Engineer, visited the Wolesley Motor Car Co.'s works in Birmingham and the NER Co.'s works in York in order to inspect petrol engines and railcars. Unfortunately, this technology was still at an early and very unreliable stage in its development, so that Mr Evans soon came to the conclusion that the steam railcar, as developed by the GWR, offered the best prospects for the ByR. However, he still advised caution, but once again his Traffic Committee was not prepared to wait, and, on 3rd March, 1904, renewed the instruction to proceed with the design of the motor car. This was soon done, with tenders then being sought and submitted to the Committee on 2nd June, 1904. That of the North British Locomotive Co., for two cars at a cost of £2,400 each, was accepted, with the option of taking a further two cars, if required, at the same price.

Consideration was also given to the question of accommodation for the new cars. On 30th July, 1904 Mr Waddell submitted a plan of a shed capable of holding no less than six cars, with room for an extension to take another two, all at an estimated cost of £2,175. This proved too ambitious for the ByR Directors, however, and on 6th October, 1904 the Traffic Committee agreed to an expenditure of £1,158 for accommodation for only three cars, and accepted the tender of Walker Bros of Walsall for the building itself, at £299. This was built in the 'vee' between the VoGR and the Barry Island Railway, adjacent to the carriage shed and served by connections off the latter line.

The first car arrived at Barry on 21st March, 1905. Although the locomotive unit had been built by the North British Locomotive Co. of Glasgow, the coach bodies, which were similar in general appearance to the later GWR cars, came from R.Y. Pickering. They seated 40 third class passengers and 10 first class, and were finished in crimson lake, the standard ByR livery for passenger carriages.

In March 1905 the *Railway Times* reported that the ByR was planning to build motor car platforms at St-y-Nyll, near St Fagans, Tonteg and Trehafod on the Barry main line, and at Fontigary, Boverton, Llandow and Ewenny on the VoGR. On 1st May, 1905 motor cars replaced trains between Cardiff and Pontypridd, via St Fagans, with platforms opened at St-y-Nyll and Tonteg. This

Barry Railway steam motor car No. 2, one of two used on the VoGR from 1st June, 1905, standing outside the motor car shed at Barry. *Author's Collection*

Class 'E' 0-6-0T No. 50, used as spare engine with the 'Motor Set' introduced on the VoGR in 1909. *LCGB*

service, putting it mildly, was not a success. There were numerous complaints about timekeeping, increased journey times and lack of accommodation, so much so that the General Manager hastily arranged for the cars to be withdrawn from the service and replaced by ordinary trains from 1st June, 1905. Tonteg Platform was closed from this date, but St-y-Nyll remained open until 18th November, 1905. The cars were transferred to the VoGR, where, from 1st June, 1905, they provided extra workings in the timetable. At this date, there were eight trains each way between Barry and Bridgend: the cars made an additional eight round trips, three of which ran as far as Southerndown Road, with the remainder turning back at Llantwit Major.

One of the advantages of motor car operation was the ability to provide additional stopping places relatively easily and cheaply. On 2nd June, 1905 the ByR Board agreed to the erection of motor car platforms on the VoGR at Fontigary and Llandow, together with one to serve a proposed golf course on Ogmore Down, near St Brides Major, the matter then being left to the discretion of the General Manager. On 14th August, 1905 William Waddell, the ByR Engineer, met the golf club committee on site, and it was agreed to locate the club house near the Pelican Inn, about 1½ miles west of the bridge carrying the Bridgend-St Brides road over the VoGR. Mr Waddell estimated that two platforms, immediately to the north of this bridge would cost about £100-£120. Nothing more was heard of this proposal or of that at Fontigary whilst on 10th August, 1905 the VoGR Board decided to defer construction of the Llandow platform until the following Spring. However, the case for this platform was then seriously undermined by a change to the line's passenger timetable: the summer service for 1906 included six cars each way, but none of these ventured further west than Llantwit Major. Without any motor cars running between Llantwit Major and Southerndown Road stations, a platform at Llandow would have had to be long enough for use by ordinary trains, something which would have led to a substantial increase in its construction cost. Nevertheless, in spite of this particular reduction the Vale timetable remained fairly lavish - too lavish it would appear. In May 1907 the ByR General Manager reported that passenger traffic on the VoGR was not satisfactory, and that it would probably be necessary to curtail the passenger service on the line.

The ByR motor cars, like others of the genre, suffered from a number of fundamental defects, such as poor acceleration and restricted access to mechanical parts. There was also a lack of capacity to cope with peak traffic demands, although, generally speaking, this was not such a problem where cars were additional to ordinary trains. The use of the cars on the VoGR gradually declined, and by August 1909 there were only two round trips left in the timetable: one Barry-Bridgend and one Barry-Llantwit Major. Nevertheless, it was clearly still felt that there was need for a more frequent service on the busier section between Barry and Llantwit Major, together with scope for operational economies between Llantwit Major and Bridgend. As a result, a replacement for the motor cars was assembled from the company's existing resources, in the form of a two-coach auto-train. The original intention was to convert class 'C' 2-4-2T No. 22 for this mode of working, but at the last minute a class 'E' 0-6-0T No. 33 was chosen instead. No.33 was one of a class of five engines built by

Barry Railway class 'E' No. 33, running as an auto-fitted 0-4-2T, at Barry station *c*. 1909.

Real Photographs

The Barry Railway motor train, comprising converted class 'E' No. 33 with the 'Motor Set' at Barry, shortly after its introduction on the VoGR in 1909. *Real Photographs*

Hudswell, Clarke between 1889 and 1891, which was generally used for shunting work. In 1909 this engine was converted into an 0-4-2T by the simple expedient of removing its rear coupling rods, although, as the rear driving wheels were retained, the technical merits of this alteration are not altogether clear. No. 33 was fitted for auto-working and piped, and, to complete the transformation, was lined throughout, with the brass dome cover polished and the chimney fitted with a copper cap. No. 53 of the same class was also converted into an 0-4-2T as a spare engine, but was not auto-fitted. No. 50 was also employed in this capacity, but remained an 0-6-0T. Nos. 33 and 53 later had their rear coupling rods reinstated.

To complete the new auto-train, two sets of coaches were formed, each set being made up of a six-wheeled brake third (Nos. 37 and 38, originally built in 1895 as all-thirds by the Gloucester C. & W. Co.) close-coupled to a four-wheeled composite coach (Nos. 152 and 157, built by the Metropolitan C. & W. Co. in 1888). A driver's compartment was provided at the outer end of the brake-third, equipped with brake and whistle controls operated by wires running along the roofs of the coaches to the engine. Regulator gear was not fitted in the coach's driving compartment; instead the driver instructed the fireman in the locomotive by means of bell signals, when operating with the coach leading.

Shortly after the introduction of the 'Motor Sets' (as they were known), H. F. Golding resigned his post as ByR Locomotive Superintendent. His replacement, from January 1910, John Auld, does not appear to have been very impressed with the rather 'Heath Robinson' mode of auto-working used with the Motor Sets. As a result, instructions were given that it should cease, and so, henceforth, the little engine was required to run round its diminutive train at its termini. The introduction of the Motor Sets had allowed a radical reorganisation of the Vale timetable, with the summer service for 1910 including only four ordinary trains each way, only two of which ventured west of Llantwit Major. Motor Sets, on the other hand, had charge of six round trips, three of which ran through to Bridgend. This was not to last, however, as by August 1911 the ordinary trains had regained their former pre-eminence, with eight trains each way, two of which terminated at Llantwit Major. Only two round trips, one to Llantwit Major and the other to Bridgend, were worked by a Motor Set.

Following their replacement by the Motor Sets, the motor cars spent much of their time at leisure in the car shed at Barry, apart from during the summer months when they were turned out to work Cadoxton-Barry Island extras. In 1914 their locomotive units were removed and the coach bodies were converted into semi-gangwayed trailers, one as a first/third class composite (No. 177), and the other as a second/third class composite (No. 178). Coupled to class 'C' 2-4-2T No. 21 or No. 22, but not auto-fitted, this train was known as the 'Vestibule Set', and was put to work on the VoGR.

World War I brought pressures for reductions in passenger services throughout the country, and by the Armistice in 1918 the Vale timetable had been cut back to five Barry-Bridgend and three Barry-Llantwit Major workings, with no Sunday service. The war years also saw the introduction of an

Class 'C' 2-4-2T No. 22 at Barry with the 'Motor Set', prior to working over the VoGR in later Barry Railway days. *C.W. Harris Collection*

Barry Railway class 'B' 0-6-2T No. 10 and its proud crew pose for the camera at Barry Sidings in the early years of this century. *C.W. Harris Collection*

operating practice which was to last until the late 1930s: the stock to form the morning through train to Cardiff was left at Llantwit Major the night before, with the engine returning to Barry and running out light in the morning to collect its train.

The working timetable for December 1921, just prior to the Grouping, reveals a complex pattern of passenger train operation, with a variety of train formations, despite the reduced service which continued in force after the return of peace. Most services were worked by the Vestibule Set, but a seven-coach set was used for a Barry-Bridgend round trip and one which ran as far as Llantwit Major, with two additional workings on Saturdays only. Another set of coaches, this time made up of eight vehicles, worked an early morning trip to Llantwit Major and back. The morning through train from Llantwit Major to Cardiff was made of seven of the 'Marble Arch' bogie coaches, which had been built by the Birmingham Carriage & Wagon Co. in 1920, and were so called because of their high eliptical roofs. Lastly, the Motor Set made a solitary appearance on a Wednesdays-only Barry-Llantwit Major working.

For most of the pre-Grouping period goods and mineral trains on the VoGR were in the hands of the engine type which came to epitomise the railways of South Wales, the 0-6-2T. The two principal classes were the 'B' class, which comprised 25 engines, built by Sharp, Stewart & Co. between 1888 and 1890, and the 'B1' class, made up of 42 engines built by Sharp, Stewart, Vulcan Foundry and S.A. Franco-Belgie between 1890 and 1900. Two engines of the latter class - Nos. 42 and 43 - were sent to Coity Shed on its opening in 1897, followed in 1900 by Nos. 39 and 108. Engines of the 'K' class of 0-6-2T, built by the Cooke Locomotive & Machine Co. of Paterson, New Jersey, and accordingly known as the 'Yankees', were generally employed on short-haul workings between the reception sidings and the coal tips at Barry.

It had originally been intended to use 0-8-2Ts on the VoGR. Six engines of class 'H' had been built by Sharp, Stewart in 1896 specially for this role, but, as they were completed before the railway opened, they were sent to work on the coal traffic of the Barry main line. In practice it was found that the 0-6-2Ts could handle the traffic effectively, and the 'H' class engines were used mainly between Cadoxton Sidings and the tips.

In 1914 the ByR introduced the class 'L' 0-6-4T, made up of 10 engines built by Hawthorn, Leslie & Co. They were mixed traffic engines, but on the VoGR they were generally used to haul coal trains between Coity Sidings and Barry, for which they were allowed (in 1914) a trailing load of up to 38 loaded wagons, compared with the 30 permitted the 0-6-2T classes. Unfortunately, this class soon acquired a reputation for derailing in sidings, the rear bogie wheels having a tendency to take the wrong road at points. The most spectacular instance of this occurred at Barry Sidings on 28th March, 1919, when No. 147 of this class, having arrived with 33 loaded wagons from Coity Sidings, left the road and fell onto its side. No.147 had to be partially dismantled in order to permit recovery to take place. Considerable difficulty was experienced owing to the lack of adequate crane power, a breakdown crane having to be borrowed from the GWR.

The 'L' class engines were also employed on the Barry-Neath goods trains introduced during World War I. In addition to these trains, the working

Barry Railway class 'B1' 0-6-2T No. 39 and the shed staff at Coity in 1908. *H.T. Hobbs*

A pause during shunting for Barry Railway class 'B1' 0-6-2T No. 112. *C.W. Harris Collection*

Barry Railway 'K' class 0-6-2T No. 121 and crew during a break from shunting duties *c*. 1905.

C.W. Harris Collection

Barry Railway class 'H' No. 84 at Barry *c*. 1905.   *C.W. Harris Collection*

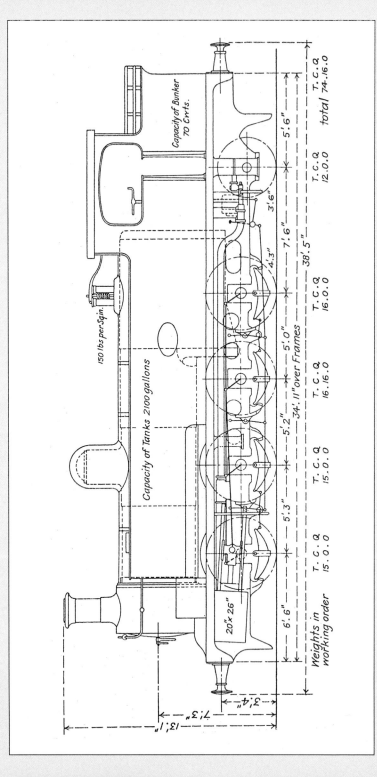

Diagram of Barry Railway class 'H' 0-8-2T.

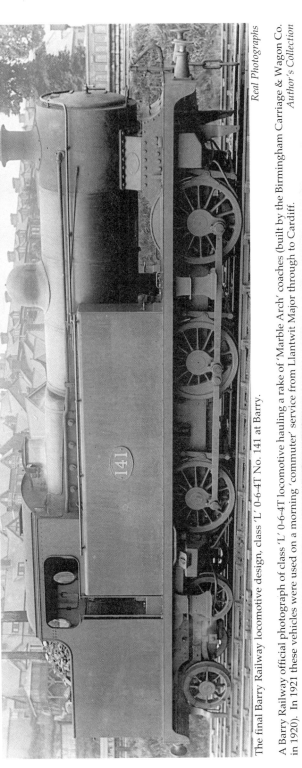

The final Barry Railway locomotive design, class 'L' 0-6-4T No. 141 at Barry.

Real Photographs

A Barry Railway official photograph of class 'L' 0-6-4T locomotive hauling a rake of 'Marble Arch' coaches (built by the Birmingham Carriage & Wagon Co. in 1920). In 1921 these vehicles were used on a morning 'commuter' service from Llantwit Major through to Cardiff.

Author's Collection

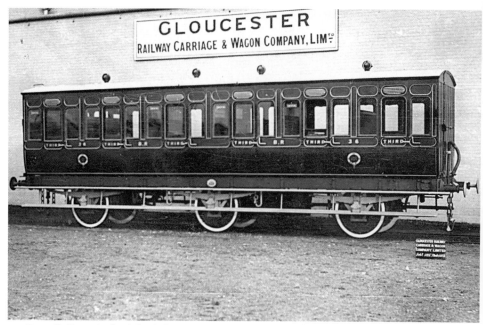

Barry Railway 6-wheel third class carriage No. 36, built by the Gloucester Railway Carriage &
Wagon Co. in 1895.   *Author's Collection*

A private owner wagon belonging to North's Navigation Collieries Co.   *Author's Collection*

timetable for December 1921 gives 14 up and 13 down empty and loaded coal trains between Coity Sidings and Barry each day. A local goods train ran from Barry to Coity, serving Llantwit Major *en route*, while another two ran only as far as Aberthaw. A cattle train ran between Barry and Llantwit Major on Mondays only.

The potential of the VoGR, coupled with the line from Barry to Cardiff, as an alternative route for trains between Bridgend and Cardiff, in the event of a blockage on the South Wales main line, does not appear to have been realised until some time after its opening. Although reference to such diversions has not been found in surviving ByR records, the trains involved would also have had to use TVR metals between Cogan and Penarth Curve. On 9th May, 1913 the TVR Traffic Committee was informed that the GWR had sought the company's permission to divert its trains via Penarth Curve and Cogan Junction in the event of a mishap on its South Wales main line. The TVR was not prepared to give an unconditional undertaking, but indicated that it would be prepared to assist in such circumstances. The TVR Minutes also record that a diversion took place on 17th December, 1916, as a result of a blockage at Pencoed, but it is not known if this was the first such occasion.

The value of the VoGR as a through route was also evident when, on 12th July, 1920, an express passenger train commenced running between Swansea and Newcastle, calling at Barry in both directions. A Cardiff-Newcastle train had run from 1st May, 1906, worked alternately with GWR and Great Central Railway (GCR) coaches. From 1st August, 1906 this service was extended to start from and terminate at Barry, with ByR engines claiming the honour of hauling trains between Cardiff and Barry. The service was withdrawn on 1st January, 1917 as part of the major curtailment of passenger services during World War I, but, on its reintroduction, it was decided to run the train to and from Swansea, calling at Barry *en route*. The first up train over the VoGR was hauled by 'Flower' class 4-4-0 No.4148 *Singapore* with GWR coaches, while the first down was in the hands of 2-6-0 No. 4310, with GCR coaches. The up train left Bridgend at 8.36 am, while the down departed Barry at 7.33 pm. Both trains ran non-stop over the VoGR, and were crewed by GWR men, with ByR pilotmen.

The subsequent history of this service is quite complex, with the train being cut back to Barry or diverted via Penarth at various periods, and is best shown in tabular form:

11th July, 1921	Up train diverted via Penarth.
3rd October, 1921	Down train diverted via Penarth.
22nd September, 1924	Service ceased to run west of Barry.
12th July, 1925	Service reverted to Dinas Powis route.
11th July, 1927	Service extended from Barry to Swansea.
24th September, 1928	Service ceased to run west of Barry.
8th July, 1929	Service extended from Barry to Swansea.
20th July, 1931	Down train diverted via Penarth.
14th September, 1931	Down train reverted to Dinas Powis route.
8th July, 1935	Up train diverted via South Wales main line.

A Vale of Glamorgan line passenger working approaches Porthkerry tunnel from the west, *c.* 1935.   *J. Hubback, courtesy John Hodge*

The down train continued to run via the VoG line until it and the up train, via Llantrisant, were withdrawn with the introduction of the emergency timetable on 25th September, 1939. In the post-war period trains between South Wales and the North-East of England have either started from Cardiff, or, if running from Swansea, have always used the South Wales main line between Bridgend and Cardiff.

During the 1920s the Vale line was also host to a number of timetabled seasonal excursion trains, which called at Barry *en route*. The working timetable for the summer of 1928, for example, gives a Mondays-only Swansea-Penzance and return working, and a Fridays-only Swansea-Shrewsbury return working, with both the up and down trains routed via the VoG line.

But to return to the immediate pre-Grouping period: the advent of GWR ownership was foreshadowed by the appearance of certain of that company's engines at Barry. In 1920 two engines of the '31XX' class of 2-6-2T, Nos. 3119 and 3140, were loaned to the ByR, and shedded at Barry. No. 119 was replaced by No. 3129 of the same class in February 1921. These locomotives were found to be capable of hauling heavier loads between Coity Sidings and Barry than was the case with the Barry Co.'s own engines. They also shared the Barry-Neath goods workings with ByR class 'L' 0-6-4Ts. Also at about this time a GWR 2-8-0T engine of class '42XX', No. 4254, was tried out on the VoGR with a train of 50 loaded coal wagons.

The takeover by the GWR in 1922 brought few immediate changes to the Vale passenger service timetable, which at that time still consisted of only five trains each way between Barry and Bridgend, with a further three as far as Llantwit Major. A late afternoon train for workmen was added between Aberthaw and Barry, and in 1924 an additional evening return working to Llantwit Major was introduced. This general pattern persisted through the rest of the 1920s and into the early 1930s. Sunday services ran only during the summer months, when there was also an extra evening working to Bridgend and back during the rest of the week. By 1935 the number of Barry-Llantwit Major workings had increased to five each way, Mondays-Saturdays.

A long-established feature of the Vale passenger service came to an end with the start of the winter timetable in September 1937. The practice of stabling the morning through train to Cardiff overnight at Llantwit Major ceased, and henceforth the train worked out from Barry in the early morning, before forming the through service to Cardiff. The approach to World War II saw the number of workings between Barry and Llantwit Major increased from five each way in 1937 to an unbalanced eight down and six up in the summer of 1939. The emergency timetable of 25th September, 1939 reduced the service by one train, each way, between Barry and Bridgend, and between Barry and Llantwit Major, but these were soon re-instated, and the pattern established prior to the emergency then continued throughout the war years. From October 1938 the Sunday service had run throughout the year, except that during the winter months it ran only as far as Llantwit Major, but from 1940 the summer service did likewise. The return of peace saw further improvement, with the summer timetable for 1947 showing six trains each way between Barry and Bridgend, with a further nine up and eight down trains between Barry and Llantwit Major.

Ex-Taff Vale Railway class 'A' 0-6-2T No. 440 (TVR No. 52) rounds the curve near Porthkerry Tunnel with a Vale of Glamorgan line passenger train, *c.* 1935.   *J. Hubback, courtesy John Hodge*

Ex-TVR class 'A' 0-6-2T No. 382 (TVR No. 160) at Barry Shed on 5th May, 1951.   *H.C. Casserley*

The years after the Grouping of 1922 saw the gradual replacement of ex-ByR locomotive classes with GWR standard types and rebuilt engines from other absorbed companies. In particular, the ex-ByR four-coupled passenger engines did not last long under the new management: the 'C' class 2-4-2T engines were withdrawn between 1926 and 1928; the 'G' class 0-4-4Ts went between 1925 and 1929; and the 'J' class 2-4-2Ts had gone by 1930. To replace these types the GWR transferred engines of the '3901' class of 2-6-2T to Barry, but these were soon replaced by former TVR class 'A' 0-6-2Ts, as rebuilt by the GWR. By 1934 there were 15 engines of this class shedded at Barry, sharing Vale passenger workings with class '56XX' 0-6-2Ts.

Although the number of coal trains passing over the VoG line had fallen in line with the decline of coal exports from Barry Docks, there were still nine such workings listed in the Working Timetable for September 1928. At this date local goods traffic required the running of three trains, one through to Coity Junction, and two as far as Aberthaw, with the Mondays-only cattle train still serving Llantwit Major. There were also through goods trains, but these usually took the form of workings diverted off the South Wales main line, to call at Barry en route, rather than services originating at Barry. In 1928, by way of example, there were two such trains: a Grangetown-Llandeilo and a Swansea Docks-Cardiff, with a third train - from Llandeilo to Roath Junction - recorded as temporarily running via the main line. All trains, except these through workings, were in the hands of engines from Barry Shed.

As with the passenger engines, the years following the Grouping saw the gradual displacement of ex-ByR goods locomotive types. Soon after the Grouping the GWR drafted in 2-8-0T engines of the '42XX' class in place of the former Barry class 'L' 0-6-4Ts, and used them on coal trains between Coity Junction and Barry. The ill-fated 'L' class soon met an untimely end, with all engines being withdrawn by the end of 1926. The reign of the '42XX' class engines on the VoG line proved equally short-lived, however, as they were soon replaced by the new standard class '56XX' 0-6-2Ts, first introduced in 1925. Engines of the former Barry classes 'B' and 'B1' lasted much longer, and continued to be employed on local goods workings throughout the 1930s. A great variety of classes was to be seen on through goods workings and diversions off the South Wales main line, with almost every class of larger GWR engine being represented, apart from the 'King' class 4-6-0 and '47XX' class 2-8-0s which were barred from use in South Wales.

As at the Grouping, the basic pattern of the passenger train timetable continued relatively unchanged after Nationalisation in 1948. It was not until 21st September, 1953 that major change came with the introduction of regular-interval services on most of the local routes into Cardiff, including that from Barry. Unfortunately, this innovation did not extend to the Vale passenger service, which continued much as before, with some very irregular intervals. There was, however, a further increase in the number of short workings between Barry and Llantwit Major, to a total of 9 up and 11 down trains. The Vale trains were also integrated with the operation of other services, such as Barry-Pontypridd, via Wenvoe, and Barry-Cardiff, via Penarth.

It was in the associated field of motive power that the new timetable

2-6-2T No. 5529 propels its auto-train out of Aberthaw for Llantwit Major in 1957.　　*R.O. Tuck*

Auto-fitted 2-6-2T No. 5527 on a passenger working in the up platform at Llantwit Major in 1957.
H.C. Manley

Ex-GWR class '56XX' 0-6-2T No. 6637 on a typical Bridgend-Barry passenger working at Rhoose station, 9th June, 1957, in the final year before dieselisation. *Michael Hale*

Barry locomotive shed in March 1958, with various 0-6-0PTs, 0-6-2Ts and the odd 2-8-0T 'on shed'. *Photomatic*

A '56XX' 0-6-2T No. 5609 leaves Aberthaw with a Barry Sidings-Coity Junction goods train on 18th April, 1957.   *S. Rickard Collection/Copyright B.J. Miller*

Class '56XX' 0-6-2T No. 5664 on an up mineral train at Rhoose on 2nd July, 1960. The 'J21' target denotes an Abercynon Shed working.   *S. Rickard/Copyright B.J. Miller*

produced the greatest change, as far as the VoG line was concerned. In September 1953 three auto-fitted 2-6-2Ts of the '45XX' class - Nos. 4578, 5527 and 5529 - were transferred to Barry Shed. Under the new regime these engines were used on various auto-train services, including Barry-Llantwit Major. British Railways Standard class '82XXX' 2-6-2Ts were also used on Barry-Bridgend trains, but the ubiquitous '56XX' class 0-6-2Ts soon came to predominate on these turns. The remaining ex-TVR class 'A' engines shedded at Barry were reduced to shunting duties and certain goods workings, but still made occasional forays on Vale passenger services. With the withdrawal of the class during 1956, surviving engines were gradually transferred from Barry to Abercynon and Cardiff Cathays sheds. Class '64XX' 0-6-0PT locomotives were also seen on auto-train services.

Class '56XX' 0-6-2Ts also dominated on mineral workings over the VoG line, but from the late 1950s 2-8-2Ts of the '72XX' were shedded at Barry for use on Aberthaw coal trains, and for banking from Barry Sidings to Rhoose. Class '42XX' 2-8-0Ts, shedded at Tondu, also appeared on workings from the Bridgend direction. On local goods trains 0-6-0PT engines of the '57XX' and '84XX' classes were the most common, although here again class '56XX' 0-6-2Ts were also used.

Excursion trains to Barry Island were always very popular, but this traffic reached new heights in the 1950s. The vast majority of these trains approached Barry Island from the east, and so did not impinge upon the VoG line. There was, in any case, a wider choice of destinations for trains from the Bridgend valleys and further west, with Porthcawl being a particular favourite. When excursions were run over the VoG line the usual practice was for them to terminate at Barry station, with passengers making their own way to Barry Island, either by the first train or on foot. This was convenient in operating terms as it avoided the need to reverse trains within the congested confines of Barry station, but was rather less so as far as the passengers were concerned.

As part of the proposed modernisation of British Railways consideration was given, during 1954 and the early part of 1955, to the introduction of diesel multiple units on passenger train services in the Cardiff District. This resulted in the publication, on 31st March, 1955, of a report entitled 'Proposed Dieselisation of Cardiff Branch Passenger Services', which included in the list of services to be operated by dmus that between Barry and Bridgend.

Derby-built diesel multiple units (later class '116') made their first appearance on the VoG line in mid-October 1957 when three-car sets were used for training purposes. They were introduced into pasenger service on 13th January, 1958, after a fortnight's delay while certain mechanical adjustments were carried out, the Vale service being operated by two- and three-car sets. A maintenance and inspection depot was established alongside Barry Island station, and the old carriage shed at Barry was also used for stabling purposes. At this stage the former steam shed at Cardiff Cathays was still in the process of conversion to use as a diesel depot.

On 27th May, 1958 ten passengers were slightly injured when one of the new dmus, forming the 5.15 pm Llantwit Major-Cardiff service, ran into the back of a Barry-Treherbert train at Barry Dock station.

The first diesel multiple unit to work to Llantwit Major on trials waits on the down main in October 1957.   *W. John Collection*

The first dmu into Llantwit Major pauses on the down main during trials in October 1957.

W. John Collection

The 11.09 am Bridgend-Barry dmu leaves Porthkerry Tunnel on 25th July, 1959.
S. Rickard Collection/Copyright B.J. Miller

A Derby-built dmu (later class '116') on the 11.09 am Bridgend-Barry service passes Barry Sidings on 25th July, 1959. *S. Rickard Collection/Copyright B.J. Miller*

A 2-car dmu pauses at the down platform at Aberthaw in the early 1960s.   *Hugh Davies*

A Cardiff-Barry Island dmu connects with a Barry Llantwit Major service at Barry on 10th April, 1964.   *R.H. Marrows*

With the development of a modern large-scale marshalling yard at Margam, near Port Talbot, from 1958, a major reorganisation of goods and mineral traffic working from the Bridgend valleys was undertaken. Under Stage III of this scheme, introduced in May 1962, all coal traffic from these valleys was taken unsorted to Margam Yard. Up to three trains each day were then dispatched from Margam to Aberthaw and Barry, the revised arrangements resulting in a considerable increase in mileage for traffic from the Bridgend valleys. Other traffic from the west, bound for the Vale line, was worked from Bridgend West to Coity Sidings by the Bridgend station pilot, in view of limited space and the operating difficulties involved in crossing the busy South Wales main line at that station. However, as a portent of things to come, traffic from the west soon began to go over to 'block' working, from pit direct to power station.

The Vale passenger train service saw relatively few changes for four years after the introduction of dmus in 1958. However, on 18th June, 1962, in an effort to reduce operating costs, the timetable was drastically reduced, the revised service offering nine trains each way between Barry and Llantwit Major, but with only three of these running through to Bridgend. As the first down and second up trains were timed for schools traffic, the Llantwit Major-Bridgend service was of little use to potential passengers, unless they wished to spend seven hours in Bridgend. The service between Llantwit Major and Barry, on the other hand, remained reasonably useful, both for work and leisure purposes, despite the reduced frequency. The most significant loss was the late evening service from Barry, with the last trains in the revised timetable leaving that station at 9.25 pm, which entailed a 20 minute wait for passengers off the connecting train from Cardiff.

During the 'Big Freeze', from late December 1962 into the early months of 1963, steam engines made a final appearance on Vale passenger workings, with class '56XX' 0-6-2Ts and three coaches standing in for the dmus, which had not taken kindly to the extreme weather conditions.

Mls.		am T	am C	am	pm	pm S	pm A	pm C	pm	pm	pm
	Bridgend dep			**9 40**			**4 2**			**7 40**	
5¼	Llandow Halt	..	..	9 54	..	..	4 16	..	..	7 54	..
7¼	Llandow (Wick Road) Halt			9 58			4 20			7 58	
9¼	Llantwit Major	6 25	8 3	10 3	1250	2 0	4 25	5 15	6 3	8 3	10 0
10¼	St. Athan	6 29	8 7	10 7	1254	2 4	4 29	5 19	6 7	8 8	10 4
12¼	Gileston	6 34	8 12	1012	1259	2 9	4 34	5 24	6 12	8 12	10 9
14	Aberthaw	6 38	8 16	1016	1 3	2 13	4 38	5 28	6 16	8 16	1013
15¾	Rhoose	6 43	8 21	1021	1 8	2 18	4 44	5 32	6 20	8 20	1018
19	**Barry** arr	6 51	8 28	1029	1 16	2 26	4 51	5 40	6 28	8 29	1026

Mls.		am	am U	am	pm	U pm S	pm	pm	pm C	pm	pm
	Barry dep	5 50	7 19	8 13	1215	1 27	2 55	4 44	5 28	6 37	9 25
3¼	Rhoose	5 58	7 27	8 21	1223	1 33	3 3	4 52	5 36	6 43	9 33
5	Aberthaw	6 3	7 32	8 26	1228	1 38	3 8	4 57	5 41	6 47	9 38
6¾	Gileston	6 7	7 36	8 30	1232	1 42	3 12	5 1	5 45	6 51	9 42
8¾	St. Athan	6 11	7 40	8 34	1236	1 46	3 16	5 5	5 49	6 55	9 46
9¾	Llantwit Major	6 16	7 45	8 40	1241	1 51	3 21	5 10	5 54	7 0	9 51
11¾	Llandow (Wick Road) Halt	..	..	8 45	..	..	3 26	..	..	7 5	..
13¾	Llandow Halt			8 49			3 30			7 9	
19	**Bridgend** arr	..	..	9 2	..	..	3 43	..	..	7 20	..

A Through Train to Aberdare (L.L.) (Tables 125, 127) **C** Through Train to or from Cardiff (Table 125)

S Saturdays only **T** Through Train to Treherbert (Table 125) **U** Through Train to or from Rhymney (Tables 131, 125)

The final Vale of Glamorgan line public timetable, 9th September, 1963-13th June, 1964, with the reduced service introduced on 18th June, 1962.

'The Leek', hauled by 0-6-2T No. 6614, at Llantwit Major on 27th June, 1964.

John Dore Dennis Collection

Passengers stretch their legs while 'The Leek' pauses at Llantwit Major on 27th June, 1964.

John Dore Dennis Collection

'The Leek' waits at the up platform at Llantwit Major while its passengers explore the station on 27th June, 1964.

John Dore Dennis Collection

Over the years the VoG line has seen many enthusiasts' excursions, but perhaps the most noteworthy was that which took place on 27th June, 1964, not long after the end of the passenger train service. Jointly organised by the Monmouthshire Railway Society and the West Glamorgan Railway Society, 'The Leek', a six-coach train, appropriately hauled by class '56XX' 0-6-2T No. 6614, ran over a number of soon to be closed lines in South Wales. Its itinerary took in Cardiff, Park Junction, Newport, Machen, Caerphilly, Pontypridd, Llantrisant, Cowbridge and Bridgend, from where it returned to Cardiff via the Vale and Barry. On the VoG line stops were arranged at Llantwit Major and Rhoose for photographic purposes.

Diesel locomotives first appeared on the VoG line in 1962, with Beyer, Peacock ('Hymek') type '3' (later class '35') Bo-Bo locomotives, which had commenced working South Wales to Paddington expresses in early March of that year, hauling passenger trains diverted off the South Wales main line. However, it was not until 1964 that diesel engines, in the form of English Electric type '3' Co-Cos (later class '37'), began to usurp steam power on coal and other freight trains on the VoG line. Tondu Shed was turned over to diesels on 20th April, 1964, before closing in October 1965, and Barry Shed was closed to steam in September 1964, although it remained in use for servicing diesel locomotives. By the end of that year the English Electric type '3s' had taken over haulage of all coal and local freight traffic on the VoG line.

For a time the short-lived class '14' 0-6-0 diesel-hydraulic locomotives were employed between the reception sidings and the power station at Aberthaw. In addition 'Hymeks' were frequently to be seen on through goods workings.

Diversion of trains off the South Wales main line between Cardiff and Bridgend has remained an important feature of traffic working on the VoG line over the years. Such diversions may result from programmed maintenance on the main line, or from an emergency such as a derailment or other incident. The value of the Vale line on such occasions is illustrated, albeit paradoxically, by an accident on 17th December, 1965, which succeeded in blocking not just the main line but also the VoG line at its junction near Bridgend station. An up empty carriage stock train hauled by Brush type '4' (later class '47') No. D1671 collided with a down train worked by an English Electric type '3' No. D6983. With both the main and VoG lines out of action, trains between Cardiff and Swansea had to be diverted via Aberdare and the Vale of Neath line. Unfortunately, this route then became blocked by a landslip on the Vale of Neath line, requiring a second alternative route, via Pontypridd, Treherbert and Tondu, to be brought into use, late on 17th December. The following day, however, this route also became blocked, this time by subsidence, leaving as the only remaining link to West Wales that via Shrewsbury and the Central Wales line. This route was used until the main line between Cardiff and Bridgend was reopened to traffic on 20th December, 1965. Earlier that year, the VoG line had proved its worth as an alternative route when, on 26th September, trains were diverted off the main line following a collision, at Llanharan, between a Swansea to Paddington express and a rail travelling crane.

'Merry-go-round' coal trains arrived in South Wales in 1966 for use on power station workings. Brush type '4' Co-Cos (later class '47') first appeared on mgr trains from Blaenant Colliery, north of Neath, to Aberthaw in 1969, and

The scene at Bridgend Barry Junction on 17th December, 1965 following the collision between a Newton Abbot-Cardiff-Neath Junction freight, hauled by English Electric Type '3' (later class '37') No. D6983, and a parcels train from Swansea, hauled by Brush Type '4' (later class '47') No. D1671 *Thor*. Both engines were subsequently scrapped.   *R.W. Ranson*

The results of a collision on 17th December, 1965 at Bridgend Barry Junction which resulted in the blockage of both the South Wales main line and the Vale of Glamorgan line. The VoG line is in the background.   *R.W. Ranson*

subsequently took over all power station traffic. A slow-speed fitted '47' was used to work mgr trains from the reception sidings at Aberthaw through the automatic unloading facility at the power station, with another member of this class banking these trains from Barry to Aberthaw. Double-heading with class '37' engines was first employed on the ash trains from Aberthaw, introduced in April 1970. From 6th August, 1979 this combination also replaced class '47' haulage on mgr trains to the power station, with the trailing load increased from 28 to 35 wagons. However, class '47' engines, equipped for slow-speed operation, were retained for unloading trips at Aberthaw, although the need for a banker was avoided under the revised arrangements.

A test train over the Ford's Factory branch, near Bridgend, on 10th January, 1980 was hauled by class '46' 1Co-Co1 No. 46 008, with the official opening train on 15th January being in the hands of class '37' No. 37 267. The first passenger working over this branch was a dmu railtour, organised by the Monmouthshire Railway Society, which ran as far as the A48 level crossing on 18th October, 1980. A similar special, chartered by the Institution of Civil Engineers, ran over the crossing and into the works sidings on 5th May, 1982. On a less positive note, the last train from Coity Yard on 22nd November, 1983 was worked by class '37' No. 37 189.

Single engine working re-appeared on the Aberthaw mgr trains in 1987 following the introduction of class '37/7' Co-Cos, fitted with slow-speed equipment and ballast weights to provide greater adhesion. The first members of this type, Nos. 37 800 and 37 801, were named respectively *Glo Cymru* and *Aberthaw/Aberddawen* at a ceremony at Aberthaw Power Station on 27th September, 1986. From 19th January, 1987, the service was reorganised with seven class '37/7', each hauling 28 wagons, in place of twelve class '37/0s', a pair of which had hauled 35 wagons. As the '37/7s' could work their trains through the tipping apparatus at the power station, the use of the slow-speed fitted class '47s' was also dispensed with.

The closure of the remaining deep mines in South Wales, after 1985, saw the emergence of new patterns of supply for Aberthaw Power Station. In particular, greater reliance was placed on opencast sources, and, from 1993, imports of foreign coal, via a new terminal at Avonmouth Dock. It had looked, at one stage, that such coal would be brought ashore at Milford Haven, a move which would have seen a great increase in traffic over the western section of the VoG line. The flow of coal from the west had declined dramatically following the closure of Blaenant Colliery on 25th May, 1990, the final Blaenant-Aberthaw mgr train conveying stockpiled coal running on 29th September of that year and hauled by No. 37 800. From July 1992 the last remaining mgr workings from the west (from Steel Supply at Neath) were diverted via the South Wales main line, Penarth Curve and Barry, in order to reduce wear and tear on the VoG line between Bridgend and Aberthaw. This left Ford's company trains and main line diversions as the only traffic on this section. This contrasted markedly with the eastern section of the line where up to 20 loaded mgr trains were timetabled each day, together with about two oil trains per week. However, the Bridgend-Aberthaw section has seen some recovery in recent years. On 8th March, 1994 the first coal was dispatched from Cwmgwrach Opencast Disposal Point, at the head of the reopened Vale of Neath branch, to the north-east of Neath. Up to six trains daily were scheduled to run to Aberthaw, some of which were routed via the VoG line from Bridgend.

A 'merry-go-round' coal train, hauled by a class '56' Co-Co No. 56 053, takes the Vale of Glamorgan line at Bridgend in 1995. *W. John*

Class '60' Co-Co No. 60 033 hauls a diverted steel coil train past the site of Llantwit Major station in 1995. *W. John*

The first appearance of a class '60' Co-Co locomotive at Aberthaw was during the night of 19th/20th May, 1991, when No.60025 *Joseph Lister* arrived with an oil train from Waterston.

Class '56' Co-Co locomotives started working mgr coal trains onto the VoG line in late 1993, with the first to reach Aberthaw Power Station being No. 56 114 assisting a class '37' from Ystrad Mynach on 26th August. On 9th January, 1995 engines of this class also commenced hauling Avonmouth-Aberthaw mgr trains, which were routed via the Severn Tunnel.

A short lived, but highly unusual working commenced on 23rd January, 1996, when class '37' No. 37 245 hauled a train of coal wagons from Pontcymmer, in the Garw Valley, to Briton Ferry, via the VoG line, Leckwith Junction, the South Wales main line and Bridgend. This circular tour was necessary because of the closure of the line between Tondu and Margam as a through route on 18th January, 1996, coupled with the lack of reversing facilities at Bridgend. However, this practice ended when a change of policy led to the re-opening of the direct link on 26th February, 1996.

Passenger trains continue to feature on the VoG line. On Sunday 8th July, 1984 a special dmu-operated passenger service, sponsored by the Barry Chamber of Trade & Commerce, was operated between Barry and Bridgend, as part of the Barry Dock & Railways Act centenary celebrations. Special trains were also run over the VoG line in connection with an open day at Barry on 19th August, 1990. The route also continues to be popular with enthusiasts' excursions. Regular diversions off the South Wales main line bring class '43'-powered high speed trains, operated by Great Western Trains and Virgin Cross Country, and class '158' (and sometimes classes '150 and '153') dmus of Wales & West Railway to the VoG line. Locomotive hauled passenger trains are very rare. Such diversions are usually timetabled for Sundays during March and April, and June and July, and are readily apparent as they require an additional 25 minutes between Cardiff and Bridgend, taking about 45 minutes for this section of their journey. Thus for about 18 days a year it continues to be possible to travel over and appreciate the many and varied charms of the Vale of Glamorgan line between Barry and Bridgend.

Diverted 'Inter City 125' takes the reverse curves at the site of Llantwit Major in 1995.
W. John

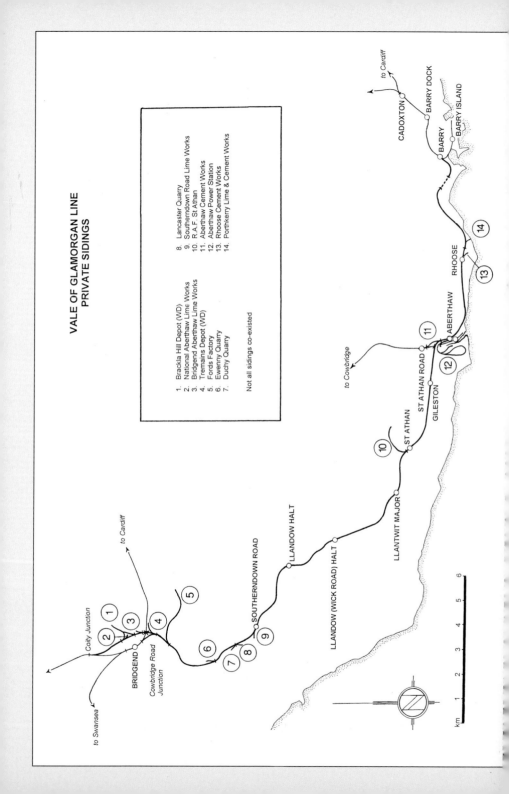

VALE OF GLAMORGAN LINE
PRIVATE SIDINGS

1. Brackla Hill Depot (WD)
2. National Aberthaw Lime Works
3. Bridgend Aberthaw Lime Works
4. Tremains Depot (WD)
5. Fords Factory
6. Ewenny Quarry
7. Duchy Quarry
8. Lancaster Quarry
9. Southerndown Road Lime Works
10. R.A.F. St Athan
11. Aberthaw Cement Works
12. Aberthaw Power Station
13. Rhoose Cement Works
14. Porthkerry Lime & Cement Works

Not all sidings co-existed

to Cardiff
to Swansea
Coity Junction
BRIDGEND
Cowbridge Road Junction
SOUTHERNDOWN ROAD
LLANDOW HALT
LLANDOW (WICK ROAD) HALT
LLANTWIT MAJOR
to Cowbridge
ST ATHAN
ST ATHAN ROAD
GILESTON
ABERTHAW
RHOOSE
CADOXTON
BARRY DOCK
BARRY
BARRY ISLAND
to Cardiff

km 1 2 3 4 5 6

N

Chapter Ten

Along the Line

Although passenger trains were withdrawn from the VoG line in 1964, it is still possible to savour its many delights as a passenger on scheduled or emergency diversions off the South Wales main line. This tour of the line, therefore, is a contemporary one, but with reference made along the route to the many features that have disappeared over the years. To avoid confusion as a result of changes which may yet occur, the past tense is used throughout. The journey is from Barry to Bridgend, with all distances, given in miles and chains, taken from Barry Junction. In railway terms this is in the down direction, the trip from Bridgend to Barry being via the up line.

Barry to Bridgend

Barry station has often been referred to as 'Barry Town', but, as far as is known, it has never carried this title. The station was opened to passengers on 8th February, 1889, on the extension of the Barry Co.'s passenger train service from its initial terminus at Barry Dock. It was originally a single platform affair at the end of a single track section from Barry Dock station, which was doubled in 1892. The station building, of timber construction, was to survive all subsequent alterations until it was replaced in the 1950s. The first goods yard, opened for traffic on 13th May,1889, was on the north side of the passenger station, in the position later occupied by the up carriage sidings. Beyond the station platform a siding ran off to serve a three-road carriage shed.

Substantial alterations were needed to accommodate the VoGR and the Barry Island line, with work starting on the former in August 1894, and on the latter in the following February. The contractors for the Barry Island line were Price & Wills, who were then also engaged on the construction of the second dock at Barry. It was necesary to remove the carriage shed, which was on the route of the VoGR, but it was not until 1st January, 1896 that the Barry Directors agreed a plan of the accommodation to be provided at the enlarged station. By the time the Barry Island line was inspected by Lt Colonel Yorke in August 1896 an island platform had been added on the down side of the station, but the track layout remained incomplete, with a simple double junction between that line and the VoGR, together with up and down bay lines at the east end of the station. Lt Colonel Yorke was particularly concerned that the new island platform was without any form of shelter, but was assured that this would soon be provided. The line to Barry Island was opened to passengers on 3rd August, 1896, and to goods on 27th January, 1897. A replacement carriage shed was built in the 'vee' between this line and the VoGR, the tender of Thomas Thomas & Sons being accepted on 5th August, 1896.

When Lt Colonel Yorke returned to make a full inspection of the VoGR in November 1897 the track layout at Barry had attained the form which was to

A Barry Island-Cardiff train arrives at Barry station behind ex-GWR class '56XX' 0-6-2T No. 6626 on 13th July, 1952. The Vale of Glamorgan line runs straight ahead.   *Author's Collection*

The complex arrangements at Barry viewed from the road bridge to the west of the station on 10th April, 1964, shortly before drastic simplification of the track layout.   *R.H. Marrows*

last through to the 'rationalisation' era of the 1960s. In addition to the double junction, already referred to, a double line of rails had been laid from the relief lines at the station westwards to Barry Sidings, crossing the Barry Island line on the level. The outer face of the down island platform was served by a line which joined the Barry Island line, to the west of the station. This arrangement was particularly useful as it allowed the down VoGR train to stand at the inner face of this platform, to await the arrival of the connecting service from Cardiff, which made use of the outer face before proceeding to Barry Island. The layout on the up side of the station was not quite so helpful, however. Here the Vale train, having arrived at the up platform, was obliged to scuttle out of the way so that the Barry Island-Cardiff train could make use of the same platform.

It will be recalled that, in August 1896, the ByR had agreed, on the prompting of Lt Colonel Yorke, to provide a shelter on the down island platform. However, this had not been proceeded with because of its high cost. With the opening of the VoGR in December 1897 increasing numbers of passengers needed to use this platform to change trains. The lack of any form of shelter provoked many complaints, but it was not until 3rd November, 1899 that the ByR Engineer was instructed to prepare an estimate for a canopy, with the tender of J. Lysaght & Co. being accepted on 3rd January, 1900.

The original wooden station building at Barry survived in increasing decrepitude until 1954, when it was demolished to be replaced by a new brick-built structure of then contemporary design. The contractor was F. Holcome & Sons Ltd. of Cardiff, the new building being opened by the Mayor of Barry, Alderman J.P. Bennett, on 28th March, 1955.

In addition to its closure proposals, the Beeching Report had also advocated the widespread recovery of redundant facilities, such as little used sidings and loops. At Barry the first to go were the carriage sidings, at the rear of the up platform, which were taken out of use on 23rd December, 1963. A major 'rationalisation' then took place between the 9th and 11th May, 1964, when the Barry Island platform line and the VoG relief lines were taken out of use, and Barry Junction signal box closed. As this preceded the withdrawal of the Vale passenger service by about a month, the last weeks of operation were subject to some operating inconvenience. This was not the end of rationalisation, however, as on 9th June, 1969 the Barry Island line was singled, although its junction at Barry remained double line. The up bay line was taken out of use in November 1972, and the crossover between the platform lines in December 1980. The canopy on the down platform was later removed, and in April 1993 the footbridge was replaced by a modern structure. The signal box (renamed 'Barry' in place of 'Barry Station' in May 1964) remains in use as the last surviving ByR feature at the station.

Barry Junction signal box was a short distance to the west of the junction itself, on the up side of the VoGR. At its inspection in November 1897 it contained 90 levers, of which 69 were in use. It was destroyed by fire on 17th July, 1907, but was rebuilt by the end of the year at a cost of £405 11s., exclusive of a new frame, which was supplied by Saxby & Farmer, and telegraph instruments. Directly in front of the box was a double line connection between the VoGR passenger and relief lines.

Class '72XX' 2-8-2T No. 7202 departs from Barry Sidings for Barry Shed, while an English Electric Type '3' (later class '37') enters the sidings in the middle distance, on 10th April, 1964.
R.H. Marrows

An up empty mineral train, hauled by class '56XX' 0-6-2T No. 5637, passes Rhoose Cement Works siding on 10th April, 1964. *R.H. Marrows*

Barry Sidings, about ¼ mile to the west of Barry station, was an important staging point in the days of the coal export trade. Traffic was worked here from Coity Junction, and then moved to the coal tips, as required. There were five sidings, situated between the up and down relief lines. The relief lines themselves rejoined the main line at 0 m. 45 ch., the junction being under the control of Barry Sidings signal box. This box was closed as part of the rationalisation scheme, carried out in May 1964, which also saw the creation of a 'down branch loop' out of sections of the old relief lines.

Just after passing Barry Sidings signal box the line entered Porthkerry tunnel (0 m. 52 ch.), 545 yds long, with portals of dressed limestone. On leaving the tunnel it ran through Porthkerry Park, curving through cuttings and over embankments to Porthkerry viaduct. From Barry Sidings to the viaduct the line climbed at 1 in 81, with the load in the days of the export coal trade, but something of a problem when coal began to be hauled, in the opposite direction, to Aberthaw Power Station. At the viaduct the gradient eased to 1 in 296, but climbed again, at 1 in 81.6, from a point immediately beyond it as far as Porthkerry West. Just beyond the viaduct was the site of a private platform that had once served Lord Romily's nearby residence. The line then passed through Porthkerry No. 2 tunnel, only 73 yds long, beneath Porthkerry Church and churchyard, before rounding a gentle curve to Porthkerry West.

Porthkerry West signal box, just over 2½ miles from Barry, had originally opened in 1898 in connection with the Porthkerry loop line. After the abandonment of this temporary feature, the signal box was retained to control a siding which was laid to serve lime and cement works, situated to the south of the line. This siding, which was provided under agreements with E.T. Ferrier and L. Alexander, was opened on 11th December, 1899. When reported on by Major Pringle for the Board of Trade on 13th November, 1900, the box contained 15 levers, all in use, and controlled, in addition to the siding connection, two crossovers between the up and down running lines. On 30th August, 1914 a new, larger signal box (2 m. 51 ch.), containing 21 working levers, was brought into use in conjunction with the opening of the new down relief line to Rhoose. The private siding agreements at Porthkerry West, latterly held by British Portland Cement Manufacturers Ltd, and the Aberthaw & Bristol Channel Portland Cement Co. Ltd, were terminated on 10th November, 1929, with the siding being removed by November 1930. With this closure and generally declining traffic, the need for the down relief line was greatly reduced. Accordingly, the junction at Porthkerry West was taken out of use on 11th October, 1930, and the relief line itself converted into a down siding, worked from Rhoose. It is thought likely that Porthkerry West signal box also closed from this date. From Porthkerry West the line fell at 1 in 165, past Rhoose cement works and into Rhoose station.

Rhoose (3 m. 26 ch.), the first station after Barry, was an uncomplicated affair, with platforms fronting the up and down main lines, and a small goods yard on the up side. The station building, of standard VoGR design in red brick with yellow brick detailing, and a gabled slated roof, stood on the up platform, with a matching waiting shelter on the down side. The station signal box was sited at the Barry end of the up platform, controlling, in addition to points and signals, the level crossing which adjoined the station.

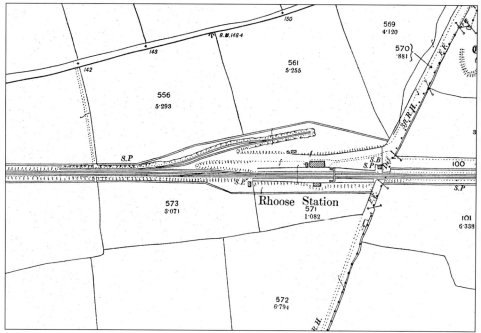

Rhoose station.

Reproduced from the 25", 1899 Ordnance Survey Map

Rhoose signal box, 30th April, 1972.   *J.A. Sommerfield*

Rhoose station looking towards Barry. *H.T. Hobbs*

The station building on the up platform at Rhoose, on 27th June, 1964, showing the extension and additional chimney at the Barry end, both constructed in 1917. *John Dore Dennis Collection*

A Llantwit Major bound dmu arrives at the down platform at Rhoose station on 10th April, 1964.
R.H. Marrows

Rhoose station with class '56XX' 0-6-2T No. 5637 on an up empty mineral train from Aberthaw Power Station, on 10th April, 1964.   *R.H. Marrows*

In September 1911 a new connection, off the down line, was brought into use to serve Rhoose Cement Works. The opening of the cement works also led to a substantial increase in traffic at the station itself. On 6th March, 1914 the VoGR Board agreed to erect a small corrugated iron goods shed on the up platform. In December 1916, in response to a further increase in business, the ByR General Manager, T.H. Rendell, recommended that the booking office be enlarged. He noted that staffing at Rhoose had increased from an agent and a porter in 1910 to an agent, two booking clerks, two porters and a lamp porter in 1916, reflecting the growth of traffic at the station:

	1910	1913	1915
Goods (tons)	21,311	64,840	106,061
Passengers	16,624	37,764	39,405

To provide this additional accommodation, the station building was extended at the Barry end by about 8 ft, matching the style of the original and adding a third chimney stack in the process.

After this burst of activity little changed at Rhoose until the closures and rationalisation of the 1960s. The goods yard sidings were taken out of use on 17th March, 1965, followed by the crossover at the western end of the station in June 1966. However, the signal box remained in use to control the level crossing gates, access to the cement works and an adjoining siding, and a crossover between the up and down running lines, until it was closed and the crossover was taken out of use on 30th September, 1978. The signal box was replaced by a ground frame, with the crossing controlled from Aberthaw signal box, the new arrangements being brought into use on 22nd October, 1978. Following the end of cement production at Rhoose in 1984, the works siding and adjacent down siding (which itself had been shortened in February 1955) were taken out of use.

Beyond Rhoose the line ran close to the coast, past Fontigary, with the gradient falling at 1 in 200. It then curved gently northwards through a limestone cutting, passing under a stone arched bridge into Aberthaw station. Just before the station the cutting to the south of the line fell away revealing a glimpse of The Leys and the mouth of the River Thaw, a view which in later years was dominated by the presence of Aberthaw Power Station.

Aberthaw (5 m. 5 ch.) was the first of three VoGR stations with platforms served by loop lines off the main running lines. The station buildings were on the up side, with the signal box centrally positioned on the down platform, next to the usual waiting shelter. A small goods yard, originally complete with brick built goods shed, was connected to the up loop line. The settlement served by the VoGR and by the terminus of the TVR line from Cowbridge was little more than a hamlet, hardly justifying one let alone two stations. Interchange between the two was not easy as the TVR station was at a much lower level than that of the VoGR, the distance by an indirect road between the two being about 600 yds. Not surprisingly many passengers, wishing to change trains, took a short cut, prompting a request from Cowbridge Borough Council for a footpath link reducing the distance between the two stations, which was accepted by the VoGR Directors on 3rd November, 1899.

An up mixed freight, hauled by 2-8-0T No. 5243, passes the junction with the Power Station branch at Aberthaw on 10th April, 1964.   *R.H. Marrows*

The simplified junction to the Power Station branch at Aberthaw in 1995.   *W. John*

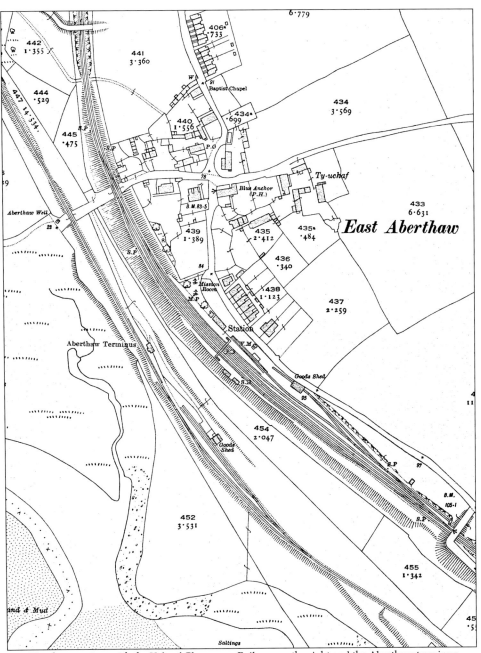

Aberthaw station, with the Vale of Glamorgan Railway on the right and the Aberthaw terminus of the Taff Vale Railway branch from Cowbridge on the left.
Reproduced from the 25", 1919 Ordnance Survey Map

A busy scene at Aberthaw on 10th April, 1964, with '56XX' 0-6-2T No. 5637 preparing to leave the Power Station sidings with an empty mineral train, while 2-8-0T No. 5243 passes through on the up main with a mixed freight.   *R.H. Marrows*

Aberthaw station and signal box, looking towards Bridgend, on 9th June, 1957.   *Michael Hale*

The station buildings on the up platform at Aberthaw on 12th July, 1959.   *R.M. Casserley*

The signal box and former down side waiting shelter at Aberthaw on 30th April, 1972. In 1997 these were the only former Vale of Glamorgan Railway buildings still in railway use.

J.A. Sommerfield

The ex-Barry Railway down starting signals at Aberthaw on 12th July, 1959.   *H.C. Casserley*

A local passenger train, hauled by a class '56XX' 0-6-2T, leaves Aberthaw for Bridgend in 1957. At this date only one line had been laid on the Power Station branch.   *R.O. Tuck*

In June 1903 the VoGR Board accepted an application from the Eddystone Aberthaw Lime & Cement Co. for a private siding connection to its works at the terminus of the Aberthaw branch of the TVR. Nothing came of this particular proposal, but it is intriguing to speculate as to how the considerable difference in levels would have been overcome.

Traffic growth, following the opening of Aberthaw Cement Works in 1913, led to the provision of two sidings off the down loop at Aberthaw. To accommodate these sidings the down platform was cut back at the Barry end, and extended at the opposite end. Application for Board of Trade sanction for these alterations was made in April 1916, but it was not until 4th March, 1920 that the new works were inspected and approved of by Colonel J.W. Pringle (this delay was not unusual in wartime).

Dramatic changes were brought about in the late 1950s with the building of the branch railway to Aberthaw Power Station. A massive embankment, wide enough for the two running lines and two reception sidings, was constructed between the station and the remains of the TVR line. The junction (4 m. 63 ch.) with the VoG line was on the up side of the overbridge to the east of the station.

The goods yard sidings were taken out of use on 4th November, 1963 and removed in December 1964. The up loop saw little use after the withdrawal of the passenger service in June 1964, but was not taken out of use until 1st December, 1966. The crossover at the western end of the station was taken out of use at the same time, but the down loop remained in use in connection with cement works traffic.

In 1981 the need to renew various track components provided an opportunity to simplify arrangements at the eastern junction with the power station line, the new layout being brought into use on 22nd/24th August of that year. This involved the installation of a single lead junction to the power station sidings, in place of the former double junction and scissors crossover. In addition, the crossover between the up and down main lines was moved to the east of the power station line junction, with a head shunt provided on the branch itself. In recent years the loop sidings on the power station branch have been spiked out of use. The original VoGR signal box has continued in use, albeit with a modern lever frame.

Beyond Aberthaw the line passed under another stone arched bridge and curved sharply through 90 degrees past Aberthaw Cement Works. The private siding agreement with the Aberthaw & Bristol Channel Portland Cement Co. was dated 14th February, 1913, and the new siding was reported to be complete and ready for inspection on 24th June of that year. Inspection was undertaken by Colonel Druitt, who recommended to the Board of Trade that approval be granted for the new works. These comprised a trailing connection from the up line to the cement works siding, and two trailing crossovers between the up and down running lines. The new connections and associated signalling were under the control of a new signal box, named 'Aberthaw West', which at inspection contained 18 levers, of which 15 were in use. The new siding continued beyond the cement works to make a connection with the Aberthaw branch of the TVR, but it was never used as a through route. A western junction

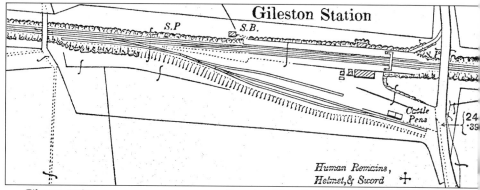

Gileston station.   *Reproduced from the 25", 1899 Ordnance Survey Map*

The rear of the station building at Gileston on 10th April, 1964. To left of the main building are the lamp room and weighbridge office.   *R.H. Marrows*

The 12.50 pm Llantwit Major-Barry dmu arrives at Gileston on 10th April, 1964. *R.H. Marrows*

to the power station sidings was brought into use on 23rd July, 1961, and took the form of a facing connection from the up line, with a single slip providing the trailing connection from the branch to the down line. On 13th August, 1962 Aberthaw West signal box was reduced to the status of a ground frame. A revised track layout, with a facing crossover and trailing connections to the cement works and to the power station line was brought into use between 23rd August and 3rd September, 1980, when the former signal box was replaced by a new ground frame.

From the cement works the line continued through the remainder of the 90 degree curve to cross the valley of the River Thaw by means of a high embankment. This was also the place at which the VoGR passed over the Cowbridge-Aberthaw branch of the TVR, with St Athan Road station on that line being visible about ¼ mile to the north. The VoG line then climbed at a gradient of 1 in 81, through a limestone cutting, towards Gileston station.

Gileston station (6 m. 44 ch.) was a simple lineside affair, with the booking office on the down platform, and a small goods yard served off the down line. The signal box was situated on the top of a cutting and on the up side to the west of the station, with a wooden framework provided in front of the box to enable point rods and signal wires to be cranked down to track level.

The goods yard layout was typical of the VoGR stations, with a loop siding, beyond which the line terminated at cattle pens and an end loading bay. A short dead-end siding was also provided. On 5th January, 1900 the VoGR Board agreed to erect a small corrugated iron goods shed, mounted on a stone-built base, in the yard. In later years the outer line of the loop siding in the yard was used to stable a camping coach. This siding was taken out of use on 30th July, 1961, but a short length of track was retained beneath the coach itself. The rest of the yard sidings were taken out of use and the signal box closed on 28th September, 1964. The yard continued to be used by a local coal merchant for many years after the closure of the rail connection.

After leaving Gileston the line ran through another limestone cutting, rising at a gradient of 1 in 82.4, before easing to 1 in 273.4 at mile post 7. From here the line continued, more or less on the surface of the limestone plateau, before curving gently to the north-west and passing through a deep cutting to St Athan station.

St Athan station (8 m. 33 ch.) occupied a very cramped site in the cutting to to the east of the bridge which carried the former main road from Llantwit Major to St Athan and Barry. A booking office was provided at road level, linked by ramps to the station platforms, on which were waiting shelters of timber construction. To the west of the overbridge was the junction with the RAF private siding and St Athan signal box (8 m. 49 ch.). The RAF siding curved sharply away from the junction and ran for about ½ mile before terminating at some warehouses and a coal stocking yard. Just before the terminus a short spur ran off to serve a brick-built engine shed. Following the closure of the private siding in 1973 the signal box was retained, for a time, as an intermediate block post for use when trains were diverted off the South Wales main line between Cardiff and Bridgend. Its closure on 19th January, 1975 left the line between Aberthaw and Bridgend as a 10 mile-long block

The station buildings on the down side at Gileston in 1964.   *Lens of Sutton*

Gileston station on 6th May, 1961, showing the canopy on the up platform built to accommodate the upsurge in traffic following the opening of RAF St Athan.   *Michael Hale*

The somewhat confusing (given that the next station was called 'St Athan'!) station nameboard
and signal box at Gileston in 1964.   *John Hodge*

Gileston station, signal box and goods yard, from the west, 10th April, 1964.   *R.H. Marrows*

St Athan station, looking towards Barry in 1964.   *John Hodge*

St Athan, looking towards the RAF siding, to the west of the station, in 1964.   *Lens of Sutton*

section, a feature which significantly limited the capacity of the line on such occasions.

From St Athan the line ran past Boverton, to the south, and then through Llantwit Major (9 m. 56 ch.) on one of the line's many reverse curves, climbing at a gradient of 1 in 106.4. At the opening of the VoGR in 1897 the ancient settlement lay to the south of the station, with fields intervening, but today the railway passes through the heart of the much larger town. Up and down platform loop lines were provided, with the station buildings on the down side, and the signal box at the Barry end of the down platform. Also on the down side, and at a somewhat lower level, was the goods yard, the largest on the line. At its opening in 1897 it consisted of the usual loop siding, but with a centrally-placed crossover allowing ready access to a brick-built goods shed on the outer line of the loop. Beyond the loop the single line terminated at cattle pens and an end-loading dock. In 1900 two short dead-end sidings were added at the Barry end of the yard. The goods yard was the scene of some exitement, on 15th January, 1904, when fire was detected in two trucks loaded with hay. However, thanks to the prompt action of the station master and the village constable, who together uncoupled and pushed away an adjacent truck, only limited damage resulted.

In the early days of the passenger service timetable all trains ran through from Barry to Bridgend. However, when first motor cars, then trains, started terminating at Llantwit Major, it was necessary for them to run forward before reversing over a crossover to the west of the station to reach the up platform. On 8th September, 1919 a new arrangement was brought into use, which avoided this operating inconvenience: a starting signal was provided at the Barry end of the down platform, which, together with the necessary facing point locks, enabled terminating trains to depart for Barry from the platform at which they had arrived.

The 1960s saw the gradual reduction and eventual elimination of facilities at Llantwit Major. The first to go was one of the short dead-end sidings in the goods yard, which was taken out of use in December 1963. Although the goods yard closed on 3rd July, 1967 it was not until 13th December of that year that the siding connection was taken out of use. However, the platform loop lines remained in place. The up loop saw very little use, but the down loop continued to be used, for a time, by trains which needed to turn back to serve RAF St Athan private siding. The loops and crossovers were finally taken out of use, and the signal box temporarily closed, on 13th January, 1969. Closure of the signal box was made permanent from 9th March of that year. The station buildings were demolished during 1968. The road through the goods yard was later redeveloped as a relief road for the centre of Llantwit Major, and to provide access to a new bus terminus on the site of the goods shed and sidings.

Beyond Llantwit Major the railway passed through a very sparsely populated part of the Vale, climbing at 1 in 106.4, 1 in 91, and then 1 in 122 to reach the summit of the line, at 253 ft above sea level, just beyond mile post 11¼. From here it began a long fall at 1 in 140, the ruling gradient for loaded trains bound for Barry, to just beyond Southerndown Road station. Soon after the summit was Llandow (Wick Road) Halt (11 m. 58 ch.), which had opened in 1943 to

Reproduced from the 25″, 1919 Ordnance Survey Map

Llantwit Major station.

Llantwit Major signal box. At its opening in 1897 it contained 31 working and 6 spare levers.

J.J. Davis

The deserted platforms at Llantwit Major, looking towards Barry, shortly after closure in 1964.

Lens of Sutton

A 3-car dmu forming the 4.44 pm Barry-Llantwit Major approaches its destination on 10th April, 1964, two months before the end of the service. *R.H. Marrows*

Llantwit Major, looking towards Barry, on 6th August, 1961. *Michael Hale*

The station buildings on the down platform at Llantwit Major shortly after the withdrawal of the passenger service in June 1964. *N.D. Mundy*

Llantwit Major, looking towards Bridgend shortly after the end of the passenger train service in 1964. *Lens of Sutton*

Right: The ex-Barry Railway down home signals at Llantwit Major *c.* 1935. *R.P. Griffiths*

Below: Overgrown, but still open to passengers, Llandow (Wick Road) Halt on 6th May, 1961. *Michael Hale*

serve a nearby RAF base. The halt had full-length platforms with rather rudimentary brick built shelters on both sides.

The line continued through rolling countryside and a series of reverse curves to Llandow Halt (13 m. 26 ch.). A signal box had been provided at Llandow not long after the opening of the line, being notified as completed and ready for inspection on 28th October, 1898, and was the subject of an inspection report by Lt Colonel Yorke, dated 6th May, 1899. The new box controlled a trailing crossover in the running lines, together with associated signalling. It was sited on the top of an embankment on the up side of the line, at 13 m. 31 ch., with a wooden framework in front of the box similar to that already encountered at Gileston. At inspection it contained 15 levers, of which 9 were in use, and its purpose was to break up the long block section between Llantwit Major and Southerndown Road. A number of ex-ByR 'somersault' signals survived at this location until the closure of the box in 1960.

Leaving Llandow the line curved once more through 90 degrees and passed into the valley of the Afon Alun, its elevated position providing advance views of Southerndown Road station. Another reverse curve brought the line into the station (15 m. 07 ch.), the third with a four-track layout. The station buildings were on the down side, with the signal box centrally-placed on the up platform. Situated in rolling countryside with very little in the way of nearby habitation, Southerndown Road was, in the days before the dominance of road transport, the railhead for a wide rural area. The goods yard on the down side of the line followed the usual VoGR pattern, but with the addition of a crossover half way along the loop siding. An additional dead-end siding was added in the early years of this century. In February 1901 an application was reported from W.H. Morgan for the lease of land in the station yard, on which he wished to build a limeworks, together with a private siding. On 5th December, 1913 the VoGR Board authorised the construction of a small corrugated iron goods shed on the down platform, at an estimated cost of £70.

Following its complete closure in 1961, Southerndown Road station was left to decay in peace for a while, and it was not until 29th September, 1963 that all points, with the exception of the up crossover, were taken out of use. The signal box was retained for use during diversions until 29th March, 1967, when the remaining crossover was also taken out of use.

After Southerndown Road station the line passed into the more rugged landscape of the carboniferous limestone country, with substantial cuttings as it attempted to follow the narrow winding valley of the Avon Alun. At 15 m. 69 ch. Duchy and Lancaster signal box was reached. A private siding agreement had been entered into with the Duchy Lime & Limestone Co. Ltd on 8th May, 1920, the siding itself opening on 13th December, 1920. It was inspected for the Board of Trade by Colonel Pringle whose report, dated 10th April, 1921, noted that the siding was served by a double junction off the main line, under the control of a new signal box, named 'Duchy Quarries'. Under a further agreement, dated 24th July, 1928, a trailing connection was put in off the down line for the Lancaster Lime & Limestone Co., the signal box being renamed 'Duchy and Lancaster Quarries' in the process. The Lancaster siding was removed in March 1953, with that to the Duchy Quarry being taken out of use

The somewhat basic facilities at Llandow Halt, looking towards Barry shortly after closure in 1964. *Lens of Sutton*

Llandow Halt after the removal of signalling and signal box, 1964. *Lens of Sutton*

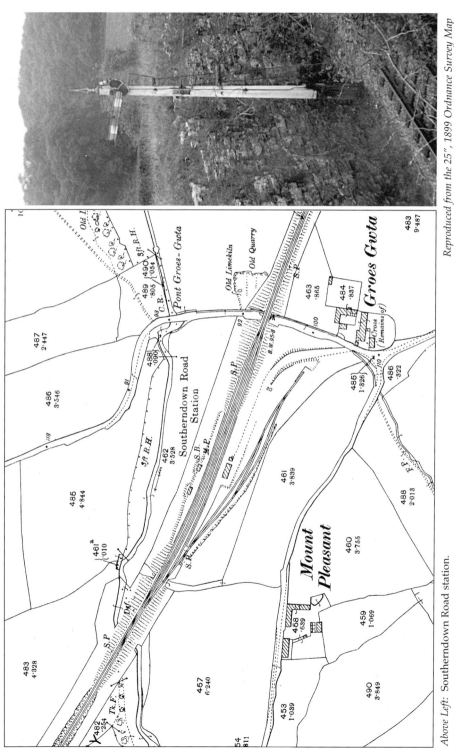

Reproduced from the 25", 1899 Ordnance Survey Map

Above Left: Southerndown Road station.

Above Right: The down advanced starting signal at Southerndown Road. The pressed metal arm retained its Barry Railway double stripe until the end.

R.P. Griffiths

Southerndown Road station, looking towards Barry on 12th July, 1959.   *R.M. Casserley*

Southerndown Road station after the removal of the platform loops and most of the signalling, 1964.   *Lens of Sutton*

and the signal box closed on 31st March, 1957.

At Ewenny the line left the hilly limestone country to cross the valley of the River Ewenni, passing, in quick succession, under the St Brides Major-Bridgend road and over that to Ogmore-by-Sea. Just before the former bridge was a siding serving Ewenny Quarry. This was one of the earliest private sidings on the VoGR, having been the subject of a report of inspection by Lt Colonel Yorke, dated 14th October, 1898. Yorke found that a new signal box (16 m. 74 ch.), containing 22 levers, of which 18 were in use, had been erected immediately to the west of the bridge carrying the road from St Brides Major. This box was closed on 30th January, 1955, being replaced by a ground frame which controlled access to the quarry siding from the down main line. This did not last long, however, being removed on 4th March, 1956.

Ewenny signal box also controlled a short siding off the down line at 17 m. 08 ch. This served a pumping station which supplied water, by pipe, to Coity Sidings, for the benefit of the locomotive department. The tender of Jenkins & Sons for the construction of the pumping station and boiler house had been accepted by the VoGR Board on 3rd June, 1896, and the siding was in place at the time of Lt. Colonel Yorke's inspection of the line in October 1898. It was removed on 6th September, 1936.

After crossing the River Ewenni, the railway curved to the north-east to follow the route of the 'Deviation Line', authorised in 1895, through a very deep cutting and under the main road from Ewenny to Bridgend. At Fords branch (17 m. 77 ch.) the branch line to Ford's engine factory, opened in 1980, left the main line, with points and signals controlled by a six-lever ground frame.

From Fords Junction the line ran in a north-easterly direction before curving sharply to the left to arrive at Cowbridge Road Junction (18 m. 35 ch.). At the junction the mineral loop line to Coity Junction ran straight ahead, almost due north, while the passenger line curved towards the north-west and its junction with the South Wales main line. Cowbridge Road Junction signal box (18 m. 44 ch.) was situated in the 'vee' between the mineral loop and the passenger lines, and contained, at its opening, 74 levers, of which 62 were in use. On 15th July, 1918 a trailing crossover was brought into use on the Coity line, near the signal box. Exchange sidings were provided on each side of the line to Bridgend station. At the Bridgend end of the down sidings was a public delivery siding called Coychurch Road Siding, opened on 1st June, 1906. Provision of this siding had been approved on 4th January, 1906, in response to an application from W.H. Morgan, the owner of Southerndown Road Lime Works, on condition that it was made available for use by the public. All the sidings at Cowbridge Road Junction were removed in December 1963, but the signal box survived the closure of the line to Coity Sidings in June 1964, to be replaced by a rather prosaic single storey structure, about 9 chains nearer Bridgend, which was brought into use on 12th September, 1965.

From Cowbridge Road Junction the line continued through the curve to join the South Wales main line at Bridgend station. This had opened as a lineside station on the South Wales Railway on 18th June, 1850, and prior to the arrival of the VoGR consisted of a down platform, on which were situated the booking offices, with an island platform on the up side, the outer face of which was used

'Castle' class 4-6-0 No. 5039 *Rhuddlan Castle* passes Duchy & Lancaster signal box on a diverted express in 1958.   *R.O. Tuck*

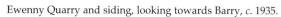

Ewenny Quarry and siding, looking towards Barry, *c.* 1935.   *R.P. Griffiths*

by trains from the Bridgend valleys. There was a small goods yard to the west of the passenger station, on the down side of the line. Immediately before its junction with the main line a single line ran from the VoG line to a bay in the down platform. A run round loop, with two sidings leading off it, was also provided in the bay. There had been a private siding off the down main line since the early days of the station, the private siding agreement with G. Jenkins & Sons being dated 22nd December, 1862. With the building of the VoGR this siding was connected to the VoGR bay line, with a crossover connecting this line to the down main line. A new signal box, 'Bridgend East', containing 61 levers, of which 47 were in use, was erected close to this crossover.

These arrangements survived largely unaltered until September 1965, when the junction with the VoG line was greatly simplified. The double junctions were taken out and access to the VoG line provided by means of a facing crossover and single lead junction off the down line. Remodelling was completed on 5th September, 1965, and Bridgend East signal box closed on 12th of that month. The layout was revised yet again in March 1978, in connection with the improvement of passenger accommodation at the station. The facing crossover, mentioned above, was removed to a new position to the west of the station, leaving only the trailing connection to the VoG line at the east end. The revised layout was completed on 10th March, 1978, and resulted in up trains, bound for the VoG line, crossing from the up line to the west of the station, and running 'wrong line' through the station to reach the VoG line. The new accommodation at the passenger station was officially opened by Nicholas Edwards MP, Secretary of State for Wales, on 30th November, 1979.

Cowbridge Road Junction to Coity Junction

Retracing our steps to Cowbridge Road Junction, today little trace remains of the mineral line to Coity Junction, which closed in June 1964. Just beyond the junction was the site of the sharply curved spur which had linked the VoG line to the Tremains Ordnance Depot. The line then passed over the South Wales main line and into a deep cutting. About 600 yds north of Cowbridge Road Junction was the site of a private siding, belonging to the Bridgend (Aberthaw) Lime Co., which was connected to the up line under an agreement dated 15th May, 1911. This siding, together with a trailing crossover in the running lines, controlled by a ground frame on the down side of the line, was opened on 24th May, 1911. The crossover was removed to a point just north of Cowbridge Road Junction in 1918. The agreement for this private siding was terminated in 1936.

About ¼ mile north of this siding was the site of the triangular junction with the line to Brackla Hill War Department Depot. The connections had been controlled by two ground frames: Brackla Hill (19 m. 05 ch.) and Brackla North (19 m. 19 ch.). In earlier days a private siding had existed just south of Brackla North ground frame, originally serving the National Aberthaw Lime & Limestone Co., under an agreement dated 4th June, 1920. This agreement, by then transferred to C.E. Lloyd, was terminated in 1936. On 10th November, 1913 a facing crossover in the running lines was brought into use, just north of

Cowbridge Road Junction on 16th April, 1960, with the Coity Junction line rising on the right and the line to Bridgend curving away to the left.

Michael Hale

this siding, which enabled the down line to be used, when necessary, for the standage of wagons, down trains then making use of the up line in order to reach Cowbridge Road Junction.

Coity Sidings, just over 19½ miles from Barry, was the place at which coal from the Bridgend valleys was transferred from the GWR to the VoGR. At the opening of the railway there were two sidings, both of which were nearly ½ mile long, on each side of the running lines. A locomotive depot, with a two-road engine shed, was situated on the down side of these sidings. The plans for this depot were dated 15th June, 1896, and it appears to have opened with the railway in 1897. However, as the ByR Co. always preferred to work its engines from Barry Shed rather than from the extremities of the system, the role of Coity Shed did not grow in importance in the years following the opening of the VoGR. In June 1906 there were only five engines shedded at Coity, requiring a staff of a foreman, two steam raisers, two cleaners and one coaler, representing a cost in wages of £6 5s.10d. per week. As the entire traffic of the VoGR could readily be worked from the Barry end, this expenditure was felt to be unnecessary, and so it was decided to close Coity Shed. Although the ByR had running powers into the GWR goods station at Bridgend, the facilities there were very limited and of course under the control of the larger company. The closure of Coity Shed provided an opportunity for the ByR to create its own goods station to serve Bridgend, and on 16th October, 1908 its Board authorised the expenditure of £1,600 for this purpose. The former engine shed was converted for use as a goods warehouse, and on 15th October, 1909 approval was given for the provision of cattle pens and an end-loading bay. The new goods station was opened to traffic on 1st November, 1909.

Following the closure of the line between Cowbridge Road Junction and Coity Sidings in June 1964 the track was lifted between the former junction and a point just north of mile post 19½. In May 1965 the layout at Coity was substantially reduced, with the former exchange sidings being converted into dead-end sidings, and the line cut back to 19 m. 56 ch. In the years that followed various other sidings were also removed.

At Coity Junction (20 m. 20 ch.) the VoGR joined the Llynfi and Ogmore section of the GWR. The GWR line was single at the opening of the VoGR: the section south of the junction being doubled on 27th May, 1900, with that to the north following on 3rd June, 1901. The junction was controlled by a standard type GWR signal box, situated 7 chains to the north of the junction. On 12th August, 1962 the line between Coity Junction and Tondu was singled, and, on 16th June, 1963, the junction itself was simplified. Coity Junction, as such, ceased to exist with the removal of the junction points and the closure of the signal box from 30th November, 1977. Henceforth, the line between Bridgend and the site of Coity Junction was worked as two bi-directional single lines: the 'Up and down Tondu branch'; and the 'Up and down Coity branch siding', with trains between Bridgend and Coity Sidings reversing at the site of Coity Junction. The Coity branch siding and the last remnant of the Coity loop line of the VoGR were taken out of use on 19th December, 1983, the day after the closure of Coity goods depot.

The former engine shed at Coity, then in use as a goods warehouse.   *L&GRP*

Coity sidings with the goods warehouse in the background, 16th April, 1960.   *Michael Hale*

Chapter Eleven

Hope Springs Eternal

The withdrawal of the passenger train service between Barry and Bridgend, in 1964, provoked continuing resentment in the various communities along the route, especially as the line remained in use for freight traffic and passenger trains diverted off the South Wales main line. The replacement bus service left much to be desired, and many former rail passengers deserted public transport altogether. In 1970 a local action committee was formed, at the request of the Finance Committee of Cowbridge Rural District Council, to pursue the possibility of reopening the line to passenger traffic. The action committee, under the chairmanship of Councillor Haydn Jones, undertook an interview survey in 2,000 homes in settlements near the railway, but as British Rail remained implacably opposed to the question of reopening, little further progress was made.

Pressure for reopening of the Vale of Glamorgan line did not diminish, however, and on 31st December, 1973 Glamorgan County Council issued a brief for a feasiblity study into the reintroduction of the passenger service. This study was carried out by Transportation Planning Associates who, in July 1974, reported to the new South Glamorgan County Council (SGCC), Glamorgan County Council having been abolished in the reorganisation of local government earlier that year. The study looked at the reopening of stations at Rhoose, Gileston, St Athan and Llantwit Major, and estimated the likely demand at about 1,100 round trips per day, of which 340 were accounted for by Llantwit Major. Two patterns of service were put forward: in one a three-car dmu was to work twice each way in the morning and evening peaks, with three round trips during the off-peak period, and one in the late evening; in the other a single car unit was to run to a similar pattern, but with an additional service each way in the peaks. In both options trains were to run, non-stop, between Llantwit Major and Bridgend. Rebuilding cost for the stations was put at £105,000, and it was estimated that both types of service would require an initial operating subsidy of £78,000 per annum for the three-car dmu and £40,000 for the single car), but that this would tail off as traffic grew, so that by 1986 the three-car dmu service would need £3,000 support a year, whilst that worked by the single car unit would be self-financing.

Public meetings were held during July 1974 at Barry, Rhoose, Llantwit Major and Bridgend, and the proposal attracted considerable local support. However, SGCC was reluctant to take on the capital cost and operating subsidy that the project would entail, and so rejected the reopening proposal. Instead improvements were made to the Cardiff-Llantwit Major bus service, which saw an increased frequency and reduced journey times.

The second half of the 1980s saw a profound change in attitudes towards local passenger services in South Wales. After the years of decline, experiments with fare reductions and improvements to frequency showed that people could be attracted back to the trains. There was also strong support emerging from the

BARRY DOCK CENTENARY

BARRY CHAMBER OF TRADE & COMMERCE

Sunday, 8th July

RETURN TRIPS DOWN THE

VALE OF
GLAMORGAN LINE

BARRY	BRIDGEND		BARRY
DEP.	ARR.	DEP.	ARR.
10.30	11.05	11.15	11.50
12.00	12.35	12.45	13.20
14.10	14.45	14.50	15.25
15.30	16.05	16.15	16.50

Tickets: Adults £2 Children & Senior Citizens £1

Available from:
**DAN EVANS   DIMONDS DELICATESSEN
E.R.C. TRAVEL   IAN HARDING
BARRY GARDEN SUBURB POST OFFICE**

Proceeds in aid of Kidney Research

BARRY ADVERTISER LTD.

Notice advertising special service of passenger trains
over the Vale of Glamorgan line on 8th July, 1984.

local authorities. Thoughts then began to turn towards expansion of the 'Valley Lines' (as the network had been termed since 1985). The Cardiff Valleys Rail Development Strategy, published by Mid and South Glamorgan County Councils in September 1985, proposed the reopening of the railway to Aberdare and a new service on the 'City Line' from Radyr to Cardiff, via Ninian Park. Under the so-called 'Speller Amendment' of 1981 to the Transport Act 1962, such services could be introduced on an experimental basis without the need for protracted closure procedures if they proved unsuccessful. This change produced a much more receptive climate for reopening proposals, and, on 28th September, 1992, Bridgend regained its former status as a junction station with the restoration of the passenger train service on the branch line to Maesteg.

This expansionist atmosphere gave a renewed impetus to the case for reopening the VoG line to passenger traffic, although the situation was complicated by a desire to provide a rail link to Cardiff Wales Airport, near Rhoose. It was always difficult to integrate this latter proposal with the reintroduction of a local passenger service over the line. However, British Rail remained unconvinced, and saw little prospect of the line covering its operating costs. In November 1989 SGCC concluded that a two-hourly service on the line would not be a viable proposition. Nevertheless, the idea would not go away, and in February 1993 the County Council commissioned a further study into the potential for reopening the VoG line to passengers. This investigation, carried out by Transmark consultancy, looked at four main options:

> Reopening of the VoG line throughout
> Reopening between Barry and Llantwit Major only
> Reopening to Rhoose only
> Provision of a rail link to Cardiff Wales Airport

In all cases the trains were to run through to Cardiff, an important principle of the Valley Lines philosophy, which had been exemplified by the success of the Aberdare and Maesteg reopenings.

Transmark found that one option, involving a 90-minute interval service between Cardiff and Llantwit Major, with additional trains in the peak hours, could eventually prove viable. This required a capital outlay of £3,600,000 and an annual operating cost of £408,000, with up to five stations (Rhoose, Aberthaw, Gileston, St Athan and Llantwit Major) being provided.

This study was subsequently overtaken by a much larger project, the Cardiff Region Transport Study, the conclusions of which were accepted by the Economic and Strategic Planning Committee of SGCC on 11th July, 1994. This confirmed the case for reopening the VoG line to passengers between Barry and Llantwit Major.

Further encouraging news came in July 1995, when it was announced that £1,004,000 from the proceeds of the sale of Cardiff Airport would be available to contribute towards the costs of re-opening the Vale line to passengers.

From this high point prospects for reopening have rapidly diminished, largely as a result of changes brought about by local government reorganisation and rail privatisation. Under the former SGCC was abolished and replaced by

A somewhat desolate scene at Aberthaw in 1995, with only one line in use at the Power Station sidings on the left, and the main lines on the right.   *W. John*

The shortened Vale of Glamorgan bay at Bridgend station in 1995.   *W. John*

two unitary authorities, one covering Cardiff and the other Barry, Penarth and the Vale of Glamorgan. Privatisation has introduced a new financial regime which has had the effect of giving much less encouragement to such reopening schemes. Rolling stock, which had previously been paid for by a capital grant, now has to be leased, while the services themselves are now liable to payment of track access charges to Railtrack. It soon became clear that under this new system a substantial and continuing subsidy would be necessary, even for the basic pattern of service envisaged. Faced with this situation and very limited resources, the new Vale of Glamorgan authority reluctantly decided not to proceed with the reopening project.

Nevertheless, hope still remains that a way will be found to enable the passenger service to be restored. Under the franchise agreement, Wales & West Railway has introduced a dedicated bus service between Cardiff Central station and Cardiff Airport, which has demonstrated that a basic demand exists on this route. The company has also undertaken a feasibility study into a rail link to serve the airport, but although this has been submitted to the national Franchising Director, it had not, at the time of writing (1997), been made public. The Railway Development Society is campaigning for the diversion of certain West Wales-Cardiff trains via the VoG line, but, to date, Wales & West Railway has not proved receptive to this idea.

In autumn of 1997 the Government embarked on nationwide consultations with a view to developing an 'Integrated transport policy'. Whether this will result in a more favourable environment for proposals for the re-introduction of passenger trains over the VoG line remains to be seen, but we must live in hope.

A six-car set, comprising one class '150' and two class '158' units, takes the Vale of Glamorgan line at Bridgend in 1995.   W. John

No. 34027 *Taw Valley* runs past the site of Llantwit Major station with the 'Tawe Taw Tourer' on 6th April, 1996. *W. John*

No. 34027 *Taw Valley* and its support coach join the main line at Bridgend *en route* for Port Talbot (to run round) and Cardiff Canton depot after developing a 'hot box' on the Vale of Glamorgan line hauling the 'Tawe Taw Tourer' excursion on 6th April, 1996. *R.H. Marrows*

Appendix One

Principal Acts of Parliament

Vale of Glamorgan Railway

52 & 53 Vict. Ch.clxxxviii: 26th August, 1889
Incorporation of company;
Four railways between Bridgend and Barry;
Confirmation of working agreement (8th July, 1889) with Barry Dock and Railways Co.

55 & 56 Vict. Ch.cxxv: 20th June, 1892
Extension of time for completion of railways;
Payment of interest out of capital.

58 & 59 Vict. Ch.xlix: 20th June, 1895
Two railways between Ewenny and Coity;
Abandonment of railways rendered unnecessary by new railways;
Extension of time for completion of railways.
Additional capital and further borrowing powers.

59 & 60 Vict. Ch.ccx: 7th August, 1896
Extension of time for completion of railways.

60 & 61 Vict. Ch.lxxxix: 15th June, 1897
Substituted railway at Coity Junction;
Extension of time for completion of railways;
Additional capital and further borrowing powers.

62 & 63 Vict. Ch.xiv: 6th June, 1899
Additional capital and further borrowing powers;
Sanction for expenditure on Porthkerry loop line.

Barry Railway

56 & 57 Vict. Ch.ccvi: 24th August, 1893
Agreement with VoGR Co.

Appendix Two

Shipment Coal Handed to
Vale of Glamorgan Railway 1897-1914

Year	Coity Junction (tons)	Cowbridge Road Junction (tons)	Total (tons)
1897	47,856	-	47,856
1898	191,573	694	192,267
1899	734,081	5,072	739,153
1900	656,263	2,712	658,975
1901	776,127	3,662	779,789
1902	840,787	6,032	846,819
1903	742,319	3,003	745,322
1904	663,630	4,981	668,611
1905	574,423	11,591	586,019
1906	660,261	26,271	686,532
1907	633,057	32,967	666,024
1908	658,649	40,055	698,704
1909	653,252	34,395	687,647
1910	672,694	35,773	708,467
1911	702,850	56,303	759,153
1912	748,709	94,261	842,970
1913	1,032,502	104,031	1,136,533
1914	1,080,729	69,624	1,150,353

Appendix Three

Loads of Engines Between Barry and Coity Junction, 11th July, 1914

Class	Type	Up laden	Empty	Pitwood
A	0-6-0T	30	50	25
B	0-6-2T	30	50	25
B1	0-6-2T	30	50	25
D (1)	0-8-0	30	50	25
F	0-6-0ST	30	50	25
H (2)	0-8-2T	30	50	25
K	0-6-2T	30	50	25
C	2-4-2T	15	30	15
C	0-4-4T	20	40	20
J	2-4-2T	20	40	20
H (3)	0-8-2T	35	55	28
D (4)	0-8-0	35	55	28
L	0-6-4T	38	63	31

Note: The term 'Laden' signifies wagons fully laden with Mineral Traffic. Five wagons of General Goods are equivalent to three wagons fully laden with Mineral Traffic. Three empty wagons are equivalent to one wagon fully laden with Mineral Traffic.

The authorised load of Up trains from Coity may be increased by one third from Llantwit Major.

(1) Nos. 92 and 93   (2) No. 79
(3) Nos. 80 to 85   (4) No. 35 and 36

Source: Barry Railway Circular No. 2,948

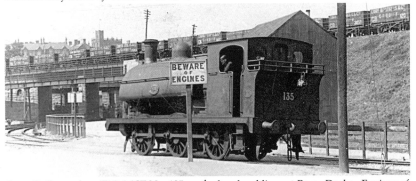

Barry Railway class 'F' 0-6-0ST No. 135 on the low level lines at Barry Docks. Engines of this type were to be found shunting at Barry Sidings and on workings between there and the tips at the docks, but were also employed on main line goods and coal traffic, as required. *C.W. Harris Collection*

175

Acknowledgements

I would like to acknowledge the help of all those who have contributed, in various ways, to the preparation of this book. Special thanks must go to Ray Caston, Tony Cooke, John Dore-Dennis, Dr Charles Donovan, Revd R.P. Griffiths, Cliff Harris, Bill John, Peter Korrison, Mike Lloyd, Bob Marrows, Brian Miller, Tony Miller, Harold Morgan, Bill Price, R.W. Ranson, Dick Riley, Chris Taylor, Ian Wright and other members of the Welsh Railways Research Circle, Historical Model Railway Society and the Railway & Canal Historical Society, too numerous to mention. Thanks too are due to my wife Diana, for her support and tolerance throughout.

Finally, I must acknowledge a special debt of gratitude for much help, encouragement and friendship given over many years by the late Iorwerth Prothero, the recognised authority on the history of Barry Docks and railways, who died shortly after the completion of the manuscript. It is to his memory that this book is dedicated.

Sources and Bibliography

This book has been compiled almost entirely from primary source material. Much has come from the Public Record Office at Kew, including Barry Railway, Vale of Glamorgan Railway and Great Western Railway Minutes, reports and other documents, and Board of Trade inspection reports. Parliamentary evidence concerning the 1889 and 1892 Vale of Glamorgan Railway Acts came from the House of Lords Record Office. Leicester University Library has provided a convenient source for Private and Local Acts, Parliamentary Notices in the *London Gazette*, timetables, journals such as the *Railway Times*, the *Railway Engineer* and the *Great Western Railway Magazine*, and the *Proceedings of the Institution of Civil Engineers*. Contemporary newspapers were mainly consulted at Cardiff Central Library, and included the *Cardiff & Merthyr Guardian*, the *Cardiff Times* and the *Western Mail*. Additional material was provided from the extensive researches of Iorwerth Prothero of Barry.

Books consulted included:

The Barry Railway, D.S. Barrie, Oakwood Press, 1962.
The Cowbridge Railway, C. Chapman, Oxford Publishing Co., 1984
History of the Great Western Railway, E.T. MacDermot, GWR, 1927.
The Locomotives of the GWR (Part 10), RCTS, 1966.
GWR Absorbed Coaching Stock 1922/1923, E.R. Mountford, Oakwood Press, 1978.
Barry Docks and Railways Vol. 1, I.W. Prothero 1995
Barry - The Centenary Book, Ed. D. Moore, Barry, 1984.
Top Sawyer - A Biography of David Davies of Llandinam, I. Thomas, Golden Grove Book Co., 1988 (first published by Longmans, Green & Co. 1938).